The Library Disaster Preparedness Handbook

John Morris

American Library Association

Chicago and London

Designed by Karen Kohn

Composed by Edwards Brothers, Inc.,
    in Garamond on a Penta Systems
    phototypesetting system.

Printed on 50-pound Glatfelter,
    a pH-neutral stock, and
    bound in 10-point Carolina
    cover stock by
    Braun-Brumfield, Inc.

Library of Congress Cataloging-in-Publication Data
Morris, John, 1912–
    The library disaster preparedness handbook.
    Bibliography: p. 1. Libraries—Security measures—Handbooks, manuals, etc.
2. Library materials—Conservation and restoration—Handbooks, manuals, etc.
3. Disaster relief—Planning—Handbooks, manuals, etc.
I. Title Z679.6M67   1986   025.8'2   86-1155
ISBN 0-8389-0438-6.

Contents

Preface

Disaster in libraries was the subject of the 1963 Library Technology Project book called *Protecting the Library and Its Resources*. It was concerned primarily with the fire and water dilemma of libraries and the need for adequate insurance. Theft and vandalism were hardly mentioned. The library today is beset by a number of concerns not considered important 25 years ago. Fire and water are still a major threat, but more versatile systems for detection and suppression of fire and modern techniques for restoration of wet books have been developed. Environmental aspects of book storage are receiving attention to slow the deterioration of collections. Thieves and problem patrons have been the subject of studies, and control measures of many kinds recommended. The science of protection of libraries from adversities is gaining strength from the experience librarians have had in dealing daily with their problems. Insurance companies have helped raise standards of protection from fire and water. Electronic systems have been adopted to control various hazards. Libraries have had difficult decisions to make in choosing between funding for collection development and user services on one hand and improved protection for collections on the other. Loss control for libraries is the substance of this book. Simple and inexpensive strategies of protection are presented along with more costly and sophisticated systems. But advice given cannot, of course, take the place of the professional judgments of consultants familiar at first hand with the situation of a particular library.

Acknowledgments

Special thanks are due the many persons who provided information and advice, particularly the following: Alice Harrison Bahr, Paul N. Banks, Sally Buchanan, Stephen E. Bush, George Martin Cunha, Pamela W. Darling, Thora L. Hutchison, Nancy H. Knight, William A. Moffett, Jean C. Morris, Mildred O'Connell, Barclay M. Ogden, Virginia Pratt, and Ed Vining.

1 | Basic Building Security

The most certain preventative to vandalism or burglary after the library is closed is a good security system. . . . Good security is still the best insurance, and is usually far less expensive.[1]

Crimes against libraries and librarians have proliferated throughout the years 1950–85. Four out of every five library fires have been deliberate burnings by vandals; rare books have disappeared from numerous libraries; and color plates and other pages have been excised from fine books. It is possible, but it seems unlikely, that the recent experience of our libraries with vandalism, theft, and incendiarism is no worse than it was in 1950, and that we have only recently begun to understand the nature of these losses and to work out defenses against them. In any event, countermeasures against library crimes and violence of all kinds are now available. But of all the precautionary measures librarians can take against such crimes, none is more basic than that of securing the building itself.

Almost all destructive fires in libraries since 1970 have been deliberately set by burglars or vandals during the night hours or at times when the library was not open. Book returns have frequently been used to torch the building. A few fires have been started by someone who broke a window and tossed a firebrand inside. Other fires have followed a break-in by burglars, thieves, and children prowling in groups. They break in where it is easiest to do so, steal what they can, and set fires before leaving. However, these and other crimes can be prevented if some basic precautions are taken to secure the library building.

General Building Security

A low level of security is common in libraries. The key to the building might be hidden under a door mat or on a window ledge instead of being given to each person who is authorized to open the building. Other errors include leaving the door unlatched or failing to close it securely; having a substandard bev-

---

1. Donald J. Sager, "Protecting the Library After Hours," *Library Journal* 94 (Oct. 1969):3609–14.

eled bolt lock or one that opens with a skeleton key; having a door lock integrated with a doorknob; having a door that opens inward and can be kicked in; and having flimsy doors or doors with large glass panels.[2] Following are some specific remedies for weak points in the building security:

> Provide double-cylinder dead bolt latching for doors.
> Eliminate any unnecessary rear door, and strengthen any service door or any concealed door that provides access to the interior.
> Provide burglar-resistant bars or grills across rear windows and across those that are concealed from the street.
> Securely bar any skylights, ducts, or small upper windows that a small person could climb through.
> Have any solvents or other flammable housekeeping materials securely locked up or stored away from the premises; similarly store tools that might be useful for forcing open locked doors and cabinets.
> Bank as frequently as possible, and keep very little petty cash at hand from day to day. Stamp checks "For Deposit Only" as soon as they are received.
> Don't put a lot of faith into having the building lighted, inside or outside, at night; lighting may only make things easier for an intruder.

The preceding recommendations are within the reach of most libraries' budgets. Where the size of the library and the value of the building and collections warrant a high degree of protection, consider installing a central station intrusion alarm system, a central station fire detection system, and a central station fire suppression system. The protection capabilities of automatic systems are explored in another chapter. Local insurance carriers and other librarians may also have good information about these matters.

Door Security

Emergency Exit Problem

Most libraries have emergency exit doors fitted with pressure-release bars (panic hardware), which cannot lawfully be chained shut or padlocked.[3] As a result, a convenient escape route is created for a book thief. It is common practice to equip such a door with an audible alarm to signal unauthorized use; but unless some staff are always in the vicinity, it is unlikely that the offender will be caught.

One method of curbing unauthorized use of a door fitted with panic hardware is to install a mechanism that delays action of the door release for 15 or 30 seconds. Such a door also would be fitted with an alarm, and the delay would give a security officer the opportunity to take action. The *Life Safety Code* permits this device to be used only in buildings that have automatic sprinkler fire protection.[4]

Another method is the use of closed circuit television (CCTV). Combined

2. Sager, "Protecting the Library."
3. National Fire Protection Association, *NFPA 101: Life Safety Code* (Quincy, Mass.: NFPA, 1985), p. 11.
4. NFPA, *Life Safety Code,* p. 11.

with an exit door alarm, CCTV surveillance allows the staff person at the monitor to see what is happening at the door. And to further improve surveillance, a video recording might be used. Either CCTV arrangement would require careful engineering to make it effective.

Magnetic Security Doors

Another promising system secures required emergency doors with a magnetic field. The door is released only for a fire or other emergency. Local fire safety authorities likely would require the release to be activated either by an automatic detection system or by an automatic suppression system for fire protection. The system also allows for release of doors from a central control point by cutting off power to the electromagnet systems. A message of instruction should be affixed to the doors to notify patrons that the doors will open only in an emergency.

It would be wise to avoid purchasing any security devices that operate on dry cell batteries, since they will frequently be permitted to lose their potency; a dead battery will not sound the alarm. This is not true of the better emergency lights that maintain power through a trickle charge from the central power supply and go into operation automatically when the regular power fails. Given a reliable product and with regular testing and maintenance, these units are dependable.

An electromagnetic locking system for doors holds an exit door shut with a 2500-lb. pull. The door releases automatically for certain emergency demands or by manual switch at a central console within the building. It may be useful in reducing unauthorized use of emergency exits. *(Photograph courtesy of Securitron.)*

Key Discipline

Key discipline is very important in helping ensure that the preceding security measures are not circumvented. It is estimated that much of the book theft that occurs in libraries is the work of insiders, staff, "familiar faces" around the library, and even faculty members. Therefore, it is good to have lockable rooms and to keep them locked. The security standards of the U.S. Treasury Department contain some useful guidelines that libraries can follow as well:

> Use only locks that have (1) multiple pin tumblers, (2) deadlocking bolts, (3) interchangeable cores, (4) serial numbers, and (5) high security ratings.[5]
>
> To facilitate detection of unauthorized locks, use only locks of standard manufacture displaying the owner's company name.
>
> Number all keys, and obtain a signature from the recipient when a key is issued. Maintain a control file for all keys. Restrict the distribution of master keys to persons whose responsibilities require them to have one.
>
> Do not issue anyone a key for access to a larger area than is necessary.
>
> Do not permit keys to be hung on a hook or left in an unlocked desk or in an unlocked room.
>
> When an employee leaves the organization, recover his or her keys.
>
> Re-key locks periodically.[6]

Bomb Precautions

If it seems unthinkable that a library could be selected by a terrorist for burning or bombing, remember that a number of college libraries were burned during the years 1965–70, and that a fire bomb was detonated in a Berkeley library in a room where students were reading. What follows are methods of detecting and reporting letter and package bombs, and ways of handling telephoned threats.

Mail Bombs

The Federal Bureau of Investigation publishes instructions on the management of mail and package bombs, including how to recognize a bomb and what to do if one is indeed discovered. They also provide good information on how to handle a telephoned bomb threat and manage a planned response to the threat of a bomb being planted in the building. Similar information should be found in each library's emergency procedures manual.

The threat of terrorist action has increased markedly in recent years, and there have been a number of bombs placed in packages and letters. These are mailed or delivered to an unsuspecting target of the terrorist. If the item is not recognized as a potential explosive message, the recipient may be badly injured

5. Laurence J. Fenelly and Louis A. Tyska, "Physical Security Standards" in *Museum, Archive and Library Security,* ed. Fenelly (Boston and London: Butterworths, 1983), p. 499.

6. John E. Hunter, "Key Control and Lock Security Checklist," in *Museum, Archive and Library Security,* pp. 535–37.

or killed. It is good to know the earmarks of parcel and mail bombs. Here are some clues provided by a British security expert:

> Parcel wrapped in reused brown paper.
> Parcel with address handwritten directly on wrapping paper.
> Parcel/letter from unexpected foreign address.
> Parcel/letter addressed in an illiterate hand.
> Parcel/letter with greasy marks.
> Parcel/letter smelling of almonds or marzipan.
> Parcel with wires or metal strip poking out.
> Parcel that sounds of loose metal when shaken *gently.*
> Parcel with springy sides (press *gently*).
> Parcel heavy for size.
> Parcel packed lopsidedly.
> Envelope with pinholes or perforations in odd places.
> Envelope stiffened with a card or with metal (flex *gently*)

If a parcel or letter is suspect:

> Put it in a safe place. Remember, it might explode before the experts get to it; therefore, put it where it cannot injure anyone and cannot damage the building.
> Call the police at once. They will not be annoyed if it proves to be a false alarm.
> Never put a suspect packet/letter in water. Explosive devices are designed to go off when opened—and water dissolves the gum holding the packet together!

Keep acquainted with current developments in terrorism. Any official announcements, especially descriptions of devices found in use, should be studied and added to this checklist. Find out who is responsible locally for advising firms about letter bombs, and keep in touch with them.[7]

Some experts recommend more conservative measures for dealing with suspect parcels. These include not shaking, pressing, testing, flexing, or otherwise handling any parcel suspected of containing explosives or other dangerous materials. The parcel should be carefully isolated for examination by a qualified ordnance disposal specialist; this is usually a function of a military organization. Library emergency manuals should have a procedure for this emergency and list the agencies to be notified. For further reading, the International Association of Bomb Technicians and Investigators publishes a concise bulletin. The U.S. Postal Service publishes similar guidelines in "Guide for Mail Bomb Security" (Notice 71, August, 1977).

Bomb Threats
However alien it may seem to one's surroundings and to one's past experience, it is possible that a library building will be the subject of a telephoned bomb threat. It is important to establish an emergency routine for handling such a call

7. Tony Hall, "Letter and Parcel Bomb Precautions," *The Bookseller* (Dec. 1974):2834.

and for taking appropriate action. Security personnel and the local police will assist library staff in setting up an emergency plan. The Federal Bureau of Investigation also issues instructions on how to handle bomb threats. Simple, understandable instructions should be put into library emergency manuals. It is very important to coach staff in what information they should try to record when they are on the telephone with a threatening caller. The Federal Bureau of Investigation has available a reporting form listing types of information that should be recorded; this form should be kept at the telephone or switchboard.[8]

Secrecy about Security Systems

It is important to maintain confidentiality, if not secrecy, concerning the security devices and systems guarding the library, especially those that protect rare books and display cases. This is the advice of Robert R. Walsh, who was put in charge of a security project at Harvard following an abortive attempt to steal a Gutenberg Bible. Walsh found that officers of banks, libraries, and museums who did not know him at all talked freely with him by telephone about their security systems. He cautions others to use extreme care about divulging details of security measures, and to make sure of the identity of the person receiving the information.[9]

8. Federal Bureau of Investigation, U.S. Department of Justice, *The Bomb Threat Challenge* (1980), p. 4.

9. Robert R. Walsh, "Rare Book Theft & Security System Confidentiality," *Library and Archival Security* 2, no. 3/4, (1978):24–25.

2 Problem Patrons

A mysterious caller informed Santa Clara that more than 20 rats, dyed red and blue, had been released in Orradre Library.[1]

Strange things happen in libraries. A fire bomb exploded in a reading room in a California library, driving out frightened students and setting off a roaring fire. In a small Louisiana library, the librarian was shot and killed by a gunman over the $20 she had in her purse. *American Libraries* reported the fatal knifing of a Norfolk staff person and the shooting of a woman security guard in Cleveland, both inside library buildings. Cleveland's downtown public library was the scene of another shooting on December 19, 1984. A mentally disturbed person shot and killed a staff worker, gravely wounded another, and also shot a female patron.

These are violent events. Yet almost daily, less violent incidents occur in libraries and create problems for staff and patrons. A wide range of disturbing scenes result from what is called "disruptive behavior," and the persons responsible for these incidents are termed "problem patrons." One library manual refers to patrons who are "disturbed or disturbing."[2] It may be inaccurate, to be sure, to describe a gunman as a problem patron. But it is apparent that coping with problem patrons of various kinds has become an area of permanent interest and concern, particularly in central urban libraries.

A telling description of the perils of the inner city library appeared in 1977. In it Carol Easton enumerates the types of problem patrons public library employees face: "drunks, dopers, vandals, knife wielders, gun toters, purse snatchers, laser-eyed paranoiacs, raving schizophrenics, lice-infested derelicts, exhibitionists, peeping toms, child molesters, and sexual deviates of every stripe."[3] Librarians tend to be too tolerant of some of these types, many of whom would not get away with their antics if librarians asserted their rights. A library cursed

1. "St. Mary's rats on S.C.," *The Santa Clara,* Oct. 20, 1983:4.

2. Judy Clarence et al., "Guidelines for Library Staff Response to Disruptive Behavior," *Public Service Policy Manual* (Berkeley: University of California, 1983), p. 1.

3. Carol Easton, "Sex and Violence in the Library, Scream a Little Louder, Please," *American Libraries* (Oct., 1977):484–88.

with such a variety of unwholesome clientele cries out for a security force to intervene for the library staff and to deal capably with these daily problems. As a minimum security watch, an off-duty police officer, preferably in uniform, could be employed. However, it is likely that today no big, inner city library is without full-time security personnel.

A Survey of the Problem Patron

To determine just how frequent, severe, and widespread are incidents involving problem patrons, a survey of 228 Illinois libraries was conducted, and the findings were published in 1981. Questionnaires were sent to large, medium, and small libraries, both public and academic. The survey solicited data on the number of disruptive incidents experienced in recent years, the nature of the disruptive behavior involved in those incidents, the staff assigned to handle such incidents, the type of guidance and training given to persons responsible for handling problem patrons, and the changes that might be made within the profession to manage the problem patron better. There was an 80 percent response rate, involving 182 respondents.

Based on these responses, the Illinois survey delineates three types of problem patrons: (1) the Relatively Harmless Nuisance, (2) the Disruptive or Threatening Provoker, and (3) the Violent Patron. Small libraries reported experiences with the first type almost exclusively. Large libraries had all three types. Violent behavior was reported by 28 percent of all libraries responding to the survey, and more than 60 percent of all large libraries reported one or more threats of arson, bombing, or other extreme violence.

The survey developed a wealth of statistical information and resulted in a number of conclusions:

Librarians are in a professional void in the absence of information on how to manage the problem patron.
Procedures for handling problem patrons are generally loosely defined or even non-existent.
Many libraries depend on unwritten but agreed-upon procedures.
Reliance on remote police or security forces is not an adequate policy.
Librarians are already handling problem situations, with or without help. They should be given training and instruction in handling problem patrons safely and professionally.

The most popular response in the survey called for the development of professional guidelines in problem patron management, as well as training programs and the inclusion in library school curricula of formal instruction in this area.

The surveyors discovered that the most glaring omission from published procedures is instruction in what to do until the police arrive. One respondent said that individual events were resolved by board action, upon which the survey team commented, "What their hapless staff did with a knife-brandishing patron until the board convened was not at all clear."[4]

A large library will depend on its security force for help in dealing with problem patron situations that are not readily resolved. Smaller libraries will refer directly to law enforcement officers and to various support agencies. Emergency telephone numbers may be listed for police departments, mental health agencies, youth services, alcohol and drug addiction agencies, and rehabilitation services. This information can be listed in the library's regular procedures manual, although many libraries prefer to develop a separate manual for dealing with problem patrons.

Dealing with the Problem Patron

Various means have been developed for managing the problem patron. In choosing a method, it is very important to gauge the behavior being displayed. Following are some behavioral traits to watch for and suggested ways of responding to them.

The Violent or Threatening Person

Don't meet the threat alone. Teamwork is the key to success, so call in other staff members or security persons at once.[5]

Do not argue with a threatening person. If no security persons are available for support, call the police.

Move away from the violent person, and alert others to move away also.

If trapped or directly attacked, shout or scream for help.

Persons who are attacked are privileged by law to use the same degree of violence in defense as is exercised by the attacker.

If necessary, defend against physical assault with total commitment and with the intent to inflict extreme pain.

Encourage library staff to become familiar with self-defense measures that can be brought to bear on an attacker.

Consider staffing various locations with more than one person at all times, thereby reducing the likelihood of physical assault on a staff member or patron.

The Angry Patron

Remain calm, not fearful. Do not become angry or combative.

Encourage the patron to talk, and listen attentively. Do not argue, no matter what the patron says.

Speak slowly, gently, and clearly.

4. J. Kirk Brashear, James J. Maloney, Judellen Thornton-Jaringe, "Problem Patrons, the Other Kind of Library Security," *Illinois Libraries* (April 1981):343–51.
5. Marion Brown et al., *Problem Patron Manual* (Schenectady, N.Y.: Schenectady County Public Library, Dec. 1981), p. 17.

Be sympathetic; try to see the patron's point of view. Express understanding by repeating and rephrasing what the patron says. However, avoid humor and personal references, and do not touch the patron.

Ask if you have stated the complaint correctly; if you have not, try again.

Continue to paraphrase the patron's statements to convince him or her that you are really listening.

When you understand what the problem is, try to take some immediate conciliatory action; offer a choice of alternatives.

If you are not having any success, yield to another staff person who may have had more experience, or who may know some way of reaching this particular patron.

Involve a supervisor or department head. If none is available, write down the name and telephone number of the patron and assure him or her that a library administrator will call.

These procedures and a firm attitude can usually calm the angry patron.

Disruptive Adults

Adults' disruptive behavior covers a wide range of antics. Such behavior is apparent and obvious when someone shouts or sings. It is only a little less apparent when patrons look toward staff members to convey a message about another patron, or stare uneasily at the patron, or get up and move to another part of the library. In such cases, several approaches may be needed:

It may be necessary to find out what is wrong, then approach the offender and explain that his or her behavior is unacceptable in the library.

If the offending behavior is not stopped at once, the offender should be asked to leave.

If the situation worsens, supervisory staff members should be informed, and security or police may need to be brought in.[6]

The Bizarre but Non-Threatening Patron

The patron who passes the time by aimlessly moving books from one shelf to another should be dissuaded from doing so, even though his or her behavior is not threatening. This is true also of patrons who exhibit erratic, illogical movements or other behavior that is distracting and disturbing to others. For these persons, the following routine is suggested:

Ask the person if he or she needs assistance of any kind. Enlist the aid and interest of another staff member.

Tell the person that his or her behavior is disturbing to others and must be stopped. Be direct and firm.

Ask the person to leave the library. If the person does not leave and the disruptive behavior continues, call the police.

Mentally Disturbed Persons

Persons whose actions or talk is disruptive and appear to mark them as mentally disturbed should be treated as follows:

6. Brown, *Problem Patron Manual,* p. 23.

Quietly but firmly tell them that their behavior is unacceptable in the library and that they should leave.

Avoid touching them.

Avoid surrounding them.

Make it easy for them to leave the building.

If necessary, get help from other staff members to talk the person into leaving the building.

As with other problem patrons, if the situation deteriorates in spite of the staff's best efforts, it may be necessary to call the police.

If the situation involves a direct exchange with the patron, follow the procedure outlined for the Angry Patron to reduce tension and to solicit the cooperation of the patron.

Above all, do not get into an argument. Maintain a pleasant, considerate, helpful, and understanding attitude.

A mentally disturbed person may require only a slightly abrasive experience to reduce him or her to desperation.

Rowdy Teen-age Gangs

Rowdy gangs require immediate intervention from staff to prevent problems from escalating. Below are some suggested approaches:

Act promptly and decisively. Approach the group and politely but firmly tell them to quiet down or leave.

Do not show fear.

Do not touch gang members.

If the group does not comply, politely order them to leave. If they show reluctance to leave, call the police. Recognize chronic offenders and identify them to the police. Failing to do so will only encourage their anti-social behavior and risk making the library the target of vandalism and further disruption.

One valuable means of managing teen-age patrons is to require them to carry a valid library card before being allowed to enter or remain in the library. This immediately identifies patrons and makes them accountable for their behavior. It also makes it easier to communicate with the teen's parents, with various youth agencies, and, if necessary, with the police.[7]

Users of Drugs or Intoxicants

Any overt use or evidence of use of drugs or intoxicants is cause for dismissal of the offender from the library. A routine is needed for easing this person out of the library quietly and without prejudice to the legal interests of the library. The procedure recommended for the Violent or Threatening Person can be followed so as to anticipate and be prepared for any adverse turn of events. If any belligerence or disturbance ensues, the police should be called in.

7. Frank J. DeRosa, "The Disruptive Patron," *Library and Archival Security* 3, no. 3 (Fall/Winter 1980):29–38.

Vagrants and Other Nuisances

The experience of large urban libraries suggests that procedures need to be developed for easing loiterers, sleepers, panhandlers, and smelly, verminous individuals out of the library. The latter types should be tactfully asked to leave if two or more patrons complain and if the staff person can confirm the complaint.

Homosexual Loiterers

A problem that is perhaps exclusive to urban public and academic libraries is their popularity with homosexuals as a place of assignation and opportunity. This activity, if not aggressively controlled, can result in a takeover of public toilets and secluded spots in the building for solicitation and sexual encounters. It is disconcerting for legitimate patrons to find a rest room haunted by one or more of these loiterers.

One student of the problem has suggested several methods for reducing this abuse and reclaiming the toilets:[8]

Practice preventive harassment, and require identification from any loiterers (in a university library, warn non-students that they can be prosecuted as trespassers).

Provide frequent tours of toilet rooms by uniformed security officers.

Knock frequently on toilet doors.

Aggressively harass loiterers to reduce the popularity of the site as an "erotic oasis."

Use the occasion of detecting persons in overt homosexual activity to spread the word about the library's hostility to this abuse of the facility. This is done through a humiliating interrogation and browbeating in a formal setting, like a security office. The interrogation is traumatic, purposefully, but tempered with kindness. No arrest is made. The process is intended to get the word out to the homosexual community that the library is determined to deny them the use and abuse of the building for assignations and casual homosexual liaisons.

In addition to pursuing a benign harassment campaign, a library staff can do some simple things along the following lines:

Provide strong, even lighting in toilets and in other places that are secluded or deep in shadow.

Remove unnecessary toilet doors, and arrange the rest room's entrance door to provide a view of the entire room as the door opens.

Remove graffiti hourly, if necessary, to interfere with cues and messages posted by consenting adults and cruising homosexuals.

Above all, regularly patrol the facilities.

The Flasher and Other Sexual Deviants

Management of this class of patron should follow procedures worked out with the best legal advice available and with the direct assistance of the police. The

8. Edward W. Delph, "Preventing Public Sex in Library Settings," *Library and Archival Security* 3, no. 2 (Summer 1980):17–26.

suggestions that follow are drawn from several sources, which vary considerably in their procedures:

> For any overt, offensive behavior, call the police at once.
>
> Get a complete description of the offender.
>
> Alert other staff members.
>
> Try not to express undue shock or alarm; deviants thrive on attention.
>
> If a staff member is directly involved, he or she may be willing to lodge a complaint with the police.
>
> If a patron is directly involved, he or she may be willing to lodge a complaint, but the librarian should not press for this action.
>
> The offended patron should be offered any needed assistance. If the patron is a young person, offer to call his or her parents.
>
> Regardless of the nature of the incident and its disposition, complete an incident report, making a record of all the details.

The Suspected Book Thief

As library workers are well aware, book theft is very prevalent. It pays to be cautious, but not overbearing. Following are some guidelines that will help curb theft yet not embarrass innocent patrons:

> When the book theft detection system indicates that an uncharged item is being removed from the library, remember that the system is not infallible.
>
> Tactfully, quietly, and cheerfully ask the patron to pass through the detection zone again so that the material causing the signal can be identified.
>
> Bear in mind that the presence of an uncharged item does not always indicate that theft has occurred; it is possible that an oversight has resulted in an uncharged item innocently being taken out in a book bag or briefcase with other books.
>
> Theft can be suspected if the book or other material is being taken out concealed under clothing.
>
> In any event, the person should be asked to surrender the book or other material.
>
> A patron can be invited to open his or her briefcase or outer clothing in the interest of discovering what is causing the theft detection system to sound the alarm.
>
> Even if theft is suspected, the suspect must not be physically detained to await the police. Detaining an individual may lead to a charge against the library of false arrest or battery.

Dealing with suspected vandalism or theft requires more than simple calm and tact. A suspect must not be subjected to a search of his or her person or clothing or in any way held up to public scorn or contempt, with or without extreme provocation. To ensure that patrons' rights are not transgressed, it is most important that librarians have a fairly complete knowledge of the legal implications in the management of undesirable patrons. The counsel of attorneys and insurers may be very helpful. A trained security staff is able to absorb this responsibility in a large library. Lacking such help, every library administration should work out with local enforcement authorities an understanding of the proper procedures to use with all kinds of problem patrons.

The Vandal

A common form of vandalism is the writing or painting of graffiti on public property. Following are some guidelines for keeping this problem under control.

Promptly remove any graffiti, whether it appears inside or outside the building. Outside, letting it remain for more than a few hours is an invitation to more graffiti and other forms of vandalism. Removing it promptly shows the vandal that you resent his or her actions and will find a way to stop them. If more graffiti appears outside, consider treating all masonry surfaces with a protective coating to make cleaning easier.

Graffiti inside the building is most likely to appear in rest rooms, usually in the form of obscene art or candid messages posted by homosexuals soliciting assignations. Removing these inscriptions hourly, as rapidly as they appear, shows the writer that his or her activities are being monitored and are unwanted in the library. Some rest room graffiti takes the form of inoffensive word games and political satire, and these should be scrubbed also, so as to discourage the practice of writing on the walls.

The Book Mutilator

Another form of vandalism is the cutting of pages, parts of pages, or color plates from a book, presumably with the intent to steal the materials. Below are listed some procedures for handling the book mutilator:

A staff member should identify the person and may later need to file a complaint with the police.

The offender may be asked to stop what he or she is doing and to speak with a supervisor about making restitution.

If the offender is obviously vandalizing books or other property with malicious intent, the police should be brought in without delay.

Detaining a Suspected Patron

The State of New York in 1982 amended the state education law to permit the detainment for a reasonable time of any person suspected of having the intent to commit larceny by concealing a book in a public library or in the immediate vicinity thereof. This legislation protects the library, its staff, and its security personnel against any action for false arrest, assault, defamation of character, and so on, that stems from an incident involving a suspected book thief.[9] Laws similar to the one that applies in New York are in effect in only a few other states.

Every library should develop its own procedures with extreme care, using sound legal counsel and working with law enforcement authorities. In addition, appropriate liability insurance should be maintained in the event of various legal

9. New York State education law, Ch. 784, Sec. 1–265, as quoted in *Problem Patron Manual*, p. 65.

actions that might arise out of the detention of a suspected thief or malefactor in the library.

Filing a Formal Complaint

It may be necessary to file a formal complaint when one is a witness to serious damage or other offenses warranting prosecution, such as theft, battery, violent

---

Tucson Public Library
Library Standards of Acceptable Behavior

Welcome to the Tucson Public Library. To better serve all library users, the Library has established certain standards. This statement of policies is intended for those whose behavior does not meet accepted Library standards. If these persons will modify their behavior, they are welcome as library users; otherwise, the Library must ask that they leave Library premises. If they refuse to leave, the police will be called and they will be prosecuted to the full extent of the law.

The Tucson Public Library System is supported by the taxes of the citizens of Tucson and Pima County, and they have the right to expect that each of the 15 facilities be a clean, pleasant, and safe building.

Libraries should be used as pleasant places to read, to choose books and other library materials, to use computers and copying machines, to attend film showings and programs, to watch puppet shows and listen to story times, and to request information from Library Staff.

Unfortunately, the behavior of a few library visitors creates problems. Behavior becomes unacceptable when it impinges on the rights of others, when it could result in injury to oneself or others, or when it could result in damage to the building or equipment. Examples of this kind of behavior include:

abandonment/leaving of young children unattended	intoxication resulting from alcohol or drugs
abuse/vandalism of library facilities or equipment	loitering, including refusal to leave at closing
bathing/washing clothes	obscene language
child abuse	sleeping
chewing tobacco	smoking
drinking	soliciting
eating	unruly/offensive behavior
exhibitionism/flashing	use of radios/TVs without headphones
gambling	use of wrong restrooms
harassment/physical, sexual or verbal abuse of other library users or of library staff	voyeurism/peeping

The following may not be brought into Libraries:

dangerous weapons
bedrolls/bed blankets
birds/snakes/animals except for seeing-eye/handidogs
drink/food

behavior, sexual assault or exposure, or destruction of library materials or equipment. A library worker who files a complaint maybe making a charge that will lead to an arrest. As a result, the worker may subsequently need to appear in a court of law to support the library's statement of the facts involved in the case. Appearing in court may be unpleasant, but it is a valuable service and is important to safeguarding the library.

Posting the Rules

It is a good idea to maintain a simple set of rules of conduct in the library, with copies prominently displayed. Doing so makes it clear that each rule is a part of established procedure and does not result from the personal whim of the library staff person concerned.

The Tucson, Arizona, Public Library posts a set of rules prominently in the library and maintains a stock of letter-size reprints. When it is necessary to call a rule to the attention of an offending patron, he or she is quietly handed a copy of the rules.

A very different style of poster establishing a standard for behavior of patrons is that of the Milwaukee Public Library, the Code of Conduct adopted in 1984. Rather than specifying offenses, it prescribes appropriate uses of the library and offers removal from the library of any person for inappropriate behavior.

> CODE OF CONDUCT
>
> *Members of the public* are to conduct themselves at all times in a manner that does not interfere with others and that is in keeping with the nature of the library's programs and services. The library provides reading areas and meeting rooms in the library building for the public to study, consult, select and examine library materials or to participate in related library programs. Any activity not connected with these purposes is inappropriate. Anyone who disregards these purposes is subject to removal from the building and/or restriction of library privileges.
>
> Adopted by the Board of Trustees
> Milwaukee Public Library System
>
> January 26, 1984

3 ■ Theft and Mutilation of Books and Materials

> *There was a reference to the bad effects of gas lighting on books at the Dane Law Library. Mr. Cutter said that when he knew anything about that library "the books did not remain on the shelves long enough to test the action of gas; they were stolen too freely."*[1]

The loss of books through theft and mutilation has something in common with the occurrence of fire in a library: until you have had a loss, you may not be aware of a problem. But with theft, unlike fire, the loss may not be realized until weeks or months after it occurs. The authors of a 1963 study of physical losses in libraries estimated an annual loss of $5 million from book theft and mutilation.[2] They reported a wide range of attitudes among librarians about these events. Some accepted them as a routine expense in operating a library and budgeted annually for the replacement of missing books. Twenty years later the estimate of these losses had risen to $50 million annually in the United States alone, "a drain on resources that translates into a threat to undermine the functioning of the research community."[3]

Types of Book Thieves

There are three kinds of thieves who steal books from libraries. The best known is the professional thief who makes a career out of stealing books and manuscripts for resale. The quintessential career book thief was James R. Shinn, and his methods were typical of the profession. He appeared in rare book rooms, typically posing as a visiting scholar or researcher. He would study the physical layout of the building, the staffing, the procedures, looking for weaknesses to be exploited for removing books. Once away from the building, he would painstakingly remove any identifying marks from the books with a kit of special tools and materials.

1. "Proceedings of the Conference of Librarians, Philadelphia, Oct. 4, 1876," *Library Journal* 1 (Nov. 1876):124.
2. Edward M. Johnson, ed., *Protecting the Library and Its Resources* (Chicago: American Library Association, 1963), p. 21.
3. "Oberlin conference on theft calls for action," *Library Journal* 108 (Nov. 15, 1983):2118.

17

He would expect to find a buyer eventually, probably one not too concerned about provenance. According to one expert on library theft, many kinds of people buy and sell books; some are reputable, some are very well established, and some operate through flea markets and garage sales.[4] Shinn was able to steal hundreds of rare books from academic libraries from coast to coast. His career ended abruptly in 1982, when he was brought to justice and sentenced to twenty years in a federal penitentiary. Since then a number of other book thieves have gone to prison. The days when professional book thieves received gentle treatment in the courts are apparently over.

Another category of book thieves are the dedicated amateurs. They use methods similar to those of the professional book thief, but they are not likely to sell the books stolen. Instead they will squirrel them away in their own private libraries. Some of these amateurs are students, pages, janitors, professors, librarians, and part-time workers employed in the library. They abuse the confidence the staff places in their "insider" status to carry out items they select from day to day. This was the habit of an instructor-counselor at Riverside, California. When finally accused, he found the opportunity to transport thousands of stolen books to a sanitary landfill, where they were duly watered down and bulldozed under layers of ordinary garbage. It is estimated that insiders may be responsible for 25 percent of all thefts of valuable books from libraries.[5]

Still another variety of thief is the one who steals a book from the reference shelves or from the general collections for convenience. Students will sometimes steal because they are too lazy to make proper use of books at the library, or just to see if they can beat the system.

The Oberlin Conference

Oberlin College Library was appropriately the site of a meeting held in September, 1983, to discuss the theft of books from libraries. This was where Director of Libraries William A. Moffett apprehended James Shinn in April, 1981. The revelation that Shinn had been able to steal nearly a million dollars' worth of books from forty libraries from coast to coast was one of the events that led to the scheduling of the two-day meeting. In attendance were librarians, booksellers, lawyers, and law enforcement officials.

Some of the statements made by participants follow:

Theft has graver consequences for libraries than does any other problem now facing them.
Librarians must accept much of the blame for losses to theft, due to their indifference, innocence, ignorance, and complacency.
Libraries are vulnerable to theft by staff members.
Prompt disclosure of book theft is the key to eliminating the market for stolen books.
Without prompt disclosure, a thief cannot be prosecuted.

4. William A. Moffett, correspondence, January, 1984.
5. "Grand Larceny," *Wilson Library Bulletin* 53, no. 9 (May, 1979):617.

According to law, if books aren't marked and thefts aren't reported, losses cannot be recovered.

The public has a right to know, even if the publicity is bad for libraries.

Libraries need a "crisis public relations" plan. They should immediately provide theft information to news media, donors, and other contacts with a need to know. However, they should avoid releasing information about the details of their security systems, about their personnel, or about their speculations on the incident.

A library should have the most sophisticated central station security system it can afford to buy and maintain.

All valued books should be visibly and systematically marked for identification as property of the library. A suitable ink for marking books is available free of charge to libraries from the Preservation Office, Library of Congress, Washington, DC 20540.

It is important not only to mark books but also to record the markings, something which may be vital in the recovery of stolen materials.

A national registry of marks and a national security office might be set up to coordinate information on book thefts for law enforcement agencies.

It is very important to develop good relationships with local police officials before a theft occurs rather than afterward. Police should be told the value of fine books and other materials in the library.

Libraries must prosecute theft or risk losing the interest of the police in pursuing thieves. More convictions and more sentences will discourage thievery. Past failure to prosecute thieves has contributed greatly to the present state of affairs.

Librarians should know the local law regarding the detainment of an individual suspected of theft or mutilaton of materials.

Only seventeen states (in 1983) had laws relating to book theft. And only nine states had laws exempting library staff from liability for detaining suspected thieves and mutilators.

Laws are needed to fill the gaps in current library legislation. One possibility would be a law holding parents responsible for damages and fines incurred by students.

Libraries are not making full use of BAMBAM, the computer-based information service on book thefts; however, book dealers are using it.[6]

The conference closed with a sense of unfinished business. The final impression was not that it was a one-time seminar, but that it was only the beginning of a continuing study of the security problems faced by libraries and of the search for more effective solutions.

It is appropriate to recognize here that the problems taken up in the Oberlin Conference were also considered in a conference at University College, London, on January 6, 1972, on "Book Thefts from Libraries." The conference was sponsored by the Antiquarian Booksellers' Association and the Rare Books Group of the Library Association. The report of the working party covers some of the

6. Gordon Flagg, "Librarians Meet to Fight Book Thieves," *American Libraries* 14 (Nov. 1983):648–49.

same ground as did the Oberlin meeting and comes to similar conclusions. There was a considerable amount of discussion about the marking of books. It was agreed that marking with inks that are difficult to remove is essential, and possibly a second invisible marking could be made that would show up only under ultraviolet light. Also mentioned was infrared fluorescence, which would not show up even under ultraviolet light, and would therefore not be discovered by a thief looking for the ultraviolet marking. A fluorescent lacquer for marking was to be tested at the British Museum and adopted for a second (invisible) stamp for marking books.[7]

Mutilation

Mutilation of library materials in its worst form is the practice of removing (with a blade or a wet string) pages or illustrations from a book. It may occur in the library or after books have been taken out. In 1976, prints of Winslow Homer paintings disappeared from libraries ranging from Maine to Pennsylvania. A few years earlier, large color prints of predatory birds and animals were found missing from books in a library of the University of California at Los Angeles. These are typical mutilation thefts, and there have been thousands of others.

A second type of mutilation, removal of pages or articles from periodicals, is primarily a problem of academic libraries. It occurs when a student is pressed for time, too lazy to make notes from the materials on the reserve shelf, or too poor to use the copy machine, and is ruthless about depriving others of the use of the materials. Users should be educated about the cost and difficulty of replacing journals, and about the utterly selfish and anti-social nature of mutilation for convenience, which deprives others of needed information. One solution is to make several photocopies of articles that are highly cited and needed by a number of users. Transferring journals to microform also has been successful. Restricting access is not a popular method, but it is very effective. Instructors can easily reduce the amount of abuse by making assignments with the mutilation problem in mind.

Although libraries' experience with copy machines has not been uniformly favorable, the provision of an ample number of good machines is considered a way of reducing mutilation incidents. But the most effective way of stopping mutilation is to observe the mutilator at work and report him or her for disciplinary action, or at the very least, for corrective instruction.

A third form of mutilation is that practiced by a thief who removes from the book the target that triggers the alarm at the check point of the electronic system. This alteration is apparently done sometimes just to "beat the system," since books thus mutilated reappear in the library from time to time.

Theft of Non-print Materials and Other Items

Many items other than manuscripts, books, and maps have been stolen from libraries. Among them were music scores, audiovisual hardware and software,

7. *Book Thefts from Libraries* (London: Antiquarian Booksellers' Association, 1972).

video cassettes, typewriters, a $3,700 OCLC terminal, and a piano. The use of fraudulent identification in the form of library cards with fictitious names has enabled thieves to steal numerous video cassettes in Ohio and elsewhere, suggesting that a picture I.D. or other verifiable I.D. needs to be required for charging out these materials.

It is likely that thefts of some items and office equipment take place during the working day, and not after hours as the result of burglary. One recommended safeguard is a scrupulous position record that keeps track of the whereabouts of all portable property liable to be stolen. Other measures that make it somewhat more difficult to walk off with portable equipment include the following:

> Painting two sides and all removable parts of equipment with serial numbers.
> Engraving I.D. numbers in two places—one not readily visible.
> Storing equipment in unmarked closets.
> Protecting the storeroom with steel doors and dead-bolt locks.
> Using posters and stamps to tell thieves that the equipment is traceable.
> Advertising missing equipment in the community.
> Installing convex mirrors to enable staff to keep an eye on the equipment.
> Using marking ink that is visible only under ultraviolet light.
> Securing calculators, record players, and projectors with locking tethers of steel cable.
> Bolting down typewriters and turntables with security hardware designed to prevent easy removal.[8]

It is suggested that the person's photo I.D. be retained when he or she is checking out these materials. The Hobbs, New Mexico, Public Library found that the solution to this recurring problem was to require a cash deposit equal to the value of the item loaned. Auto repair manuals used to disappear routinely under the honor system, but under the cash deposit system, they always come back.

A library should adopt whatever system or combination of procedures provides security for that particular library. It is absurd to debate systems on moral grounds or to debate whether a system of preventing theft uses a positive or negative approach. What counts is a commitment on the part of the library staff and the user community to doing something effective.

Other Ways to Prevent Theft and Mutilation

Security Personnel and Procedures

Thefts, mutilations, and various aberrations of problem patrons are best controlled through purposeful surveillance, either directly or through closed circuit television. Very large libraries, particularly in urban centers, may need to employ full-time security forces. Boston Public Library, for example, uses a two-level security force: a corps of internal security guards (inspection and information personnel) backed up by a national security organization. The internal guards

8. Herbert Katzenstein, "Guidelines for Security of AV Equipment," *Library Security Newsletter* 1 (July 1975):9.

function as a protection system, and the national company guards are the enforcement officers. When a troublesome patron or a suspected thief needs to be interrogated or taken into custody, he or she is transferred to the national security service. Internal guards do the checking of briefcases and bags at the exits to make sure that uncharged books or other materials are not removed from the library. Both types of guards work inside the library.

One advantage of employing internal security people is the possibility of having them perform incidental library work (as a means of surveillance), but not to the extent of lessening their contribution to security. Contract guard services are now available almost everywhere, but it is wise to go slowly in making any contractual arrangement. Not all guards are highly trained and capable of handling every situation. Moreover, the library should retain some degree of selectivity even under the contract. Also be aware that regional and local security companies may not be as well organized and regulated in some areas as they are in others. Even the well-known, national security organizations have had problems with trigger-happy and thieving guards in their employ.

Security Staff   The Milwaukee Public Library at one time had staff members wearing badges with the legend "May I Help You?" They now use a badge showing the logotype of the library. This makes it easy for the uniformed security guards to distinguish them from patrons in maintaining security of some areas in the library. Another library has made use of frequent patrols of the stacks by staffers who speak to patrons and offer assistance, showing that the library cares about them and about its materials. These practices suggest that surveillance can be carried out unobtrusively as an adjunct to conventional library work routines and, conversely, that part-time security persons can carry out library duties that are compatible with, but incidental to, their primary function.

A large library can employ a professional security staff that is carefully selected, well trained, and capable of cordial and friendly conversation with patrons. These considerations are particularly valuable in making patrons more conscious of security problems. Small libraries that lack funding for security staff may be able to arrange for routine visits by uniformed police during hours of recurring stress from problem patrons. These visits would strengthen library-police relationships and would have a beneficial effect on security generally.

Book Theft Detection Systems

Electronic thief detection systems placed at the point where patrons charge out books have become increasingly popular for preventing the theft of books from libraries. Yet they are not foolproof. They can be evaded by determined thieves and cheaters and they are inadequate to the task of protecting rare books and manuscripts. But in protecting the general collections and in reminding absent-minded patrons to present books for charging, they are judged 75 to 95 percent effective.[9]

The decision to invest in an electronic system should be based on the needs of the individual library, and the capabilities of various systems should be examined to determine which system best matches those needs. A book census or

9. Alice Harrison Bahr, *Book Theft and Library Security Systems 1981–82* (White Plains: Knowledge Industry Publications, 1981), 5.

sample can be taken to determine the loss ratio. Another alternative is to take inventory, which will determine loss and accomplish other tasks at the same time. This approach is slower and more costly than the first, but if the library can be shut down for a brief interval, it is possible for regular staff and only a few assistants to take inventory.

When choosing a system, keep in mind the following points. The electronic system is one of several basic security measures. It creates an illusion of security, it informs patrons that the library is trying to reduce losses to theft, and it prevents inadvertent removal of uncharged items. All electronic book theft detection systems can operate as bypass or full circulating systems, which means that materials can either be passed around or carried through system-sensing screens. Both systems rely on the presence in the book of a metallic target that will alert the staff through a visual or audible signal that a book not properly charged is moving through the gate. This system is adequate for discovering the innocent oversight of a patron carrying an uncharged item, but it is only a challenge for the calculating thief, who may remove the target while inside the library and carry the book out, concealed or not, depending on the nature of the charge-out procedure. The thief may choose to leave the target intact and carry the book past the gate by holding it in an inert position, or by sliding it along the floor, or by securing the help of an accomplice in a library where this is possible.

Although these systems can be thwarted by determined thieves, they nonetheless serve an important security function. Consider the following facts: every system has reduced the number of books lost to theft, in some instances by as much as 85 percent; and only a few libraries have used electronic checkout systems and then abandoned them entirely.[10]

Moreover, book theft detection systems continue to improve. In 1984, a plug-in radio frequency system was introduced. This system offers double-corridor protection ranging from six to eight feet using a single screen, and it is considerably less expensive than earlier systems. Radio frequency detection also is thought to create fewer false alarms than other systems, and it avoids the loss of data from audio, video, and computer tapes, such as may be experienced with electro-magnetic detection in the full circulating mode.

The use of similar systems in retail stores, a much larger market, also has aided the development of library systems and has doubtless helped with their acceptance by patrons. Further improvements are expected. These include the placing of screens overhead and in the floor, as has already been done in stores. Additionally, more streamlined and portable equipment of benefit to small and specialized libraries can be expected. Finally, systems without gates or turnstiles are already in use, but it is often difficult to determine which person in a group may have triggered the alarm, and thus several may have to be asked to pass through the system again.

Investment in an electronic system can be justified when the predicted savings in losses over a period of several years equals the cost of the installation. For a large library that has a substantial annual loss and a single checkout point, the installation of an electronic system would likely be a good investment.

10. Alice Harrison Bahr, correspondence, December, 1985.

A book theft detection system obtaining a double corridor of protection from a single panel. *(Photograph courtesy of the 3M Company.)*

Purchasing an Electronic Theft Detection System   Surveys conducted of theft detection systems over a number of years cited several points a library should consider before purchasing such a system:

Some equipment is suitable for monitoring bound books only.

Some targets are more concealable than others, hence more resistant to compromise through tampering. For instance, tape targets are more concealable than label targets, but they take about four times as long to install. This is because care is needed in inserting tape strip targets to avoid damaging the turn-up or cuff of the spine.

Volumes of multiple periodical issues can be protected fairly easily through the use of the "perfect" adhesive binding.

Target labels are available that have a low acid content and an adhesive with similar characteristics.

The sensitivity of alarm systems must be easily adjustable to reduce false alarms or, conversely, failure to detect targets.

The aisle width required varies from 18 to 36 inches, and even more for some newer systems.

Electrical power requirements may demand additional wiring.

Some trouble is possible through the juxtaposition of incompatible electrical systems, as may happen when electromagnetic detection is introduced too close to automated circulation control system terminals.

Some equipment is not compatible with magnetic tapes for cassette or reel-

Detection systems are being constantly improved. A recent development is 3M's Echotag Book Detection System, described as an affordable system designed for small- and medium-sized libraries. It can operate with a single outporte detection panel or with two panels flanking a 6-foot double-door exit, as in the Glencove, N.Y., Public Library, shown here. *(Photograph courtesy of the 3M Company.)*

to-reel devices in that the contents of a tape may be destroyed by a deactivating unit.

All manufacturers provide maintenance service, but the quality of service varies from one manufacturer to another. The experience of other local libraries may be the best indicator of what kind of service can be expected. (All manufacturers provide lists of users of their equipment, making it possible to check with other libraries for first-hand information about service, repairs, and other points of interest.)[11]

Turnstiles

Guarded mechanical (non-electronic) turnstiles also have been widely used at checkout points and are considered beneficial, but they are effective only if every book that goes out is actually checked by an attendant. Therefore, a large crowd must not be permitted to file out rapidly, as happens at closing time, without each person being checked. The staff's failure to look into purses and briefcases is another weak point in this system, as is the difficulty of sensing whether some-

11. Nancy H. Knight, "Theft Detection Systems for Libraries Revisited, An Updated Survey," *Library Technology Reports* 15 (May/June 1979):3.

one has concealed a book in clothing. Thieves are alert to such weaknesses in procedure and will take advantage of them.

Closed Circuit Television

Closed circuit television (CCTV) is yet another device that can perform valuable security services. The large downtown library is probably the ideal candidate for CCTV use. Small libraries generally are better served by electronic theft detection systems, especially if adequate staff are not available to spend time at the monitor.

The best CCTV systems employ zoom lenses, which give sharp resolution to a smaller field than does a fixed focal length lens, but zoom lenses are expensive. A motorized zoom lens makes it possible to examine closely a portion of the field being monitored. Pan-tilt action of the camera is another extra feature that gives a greater dimension to CCTV, as do low light lenses, some of which can operate in darkness. However, using a low light lens is costlier than stepping up the room lighting, and the latter improvement probably will produce a better image. Finally, video taping of the image picked up by the camera is possible and allows staff to review in a short time a lengthy period of recording. This is especially valuable in identifying persons who make illicit use of emergency exits.

Whatever CCTV system is used, don't expect too much from it. Keep in mind that the attention span of a watcher is about twenty minutes, and this duty should be rotated accordingly.

Restricted Access

William A. Moffett has observed a close correlation between the growing awareness of security problems in libraries and the disappearance of closed stacks in the design of library buildings.[12] However, when the University of Toronto's new research library was preparing to operate with closed stacks, a raucous student demonstration of protest ensued, with the faculty eventually conceding student access on the basis of "academic need." Libraries in British and European universities, except Cambridge, uniformly have closed stacks. In a number of libraries in this country as well, closed stack procedures are replacing the so-called American way of keeping everything on open shelves. Reserve systems are effective, and locked cases are needed for some materials.

The Special Problem of Protecting Rare Books and Manuscripts   Restricted access is given full play in the rare book room and in special collections, areas where the most solemn trust of the librarian is at the same time the quarry of the thief. The bitter experience of many libraries with theft of fine books and other things suggests that these precautions are appropriate:

> Make a scrupulous check of all the identification data presented by an unknown person who asks to have access to valued materials. This single procedure, pursued aggressively, would have prevented various earlier thefts.

12. Correspondence, February, 1984.

When a casual visitor wants to examine a prized manuscript, offer a photocopy instead of the original.

Maintain a precise record of manuscripts and small items so that each is described individually (not "Hemingway, E., 5 items," which makes it easy for a thief to exchange a spurious item for the real one).

With rare or special collections materials that are kept in folders, permit a patron to have only one folder at one time. Count the folder items when they are given to the patron, and again when they are returned. Even better, offer the patron only one item at a time.

Evaluate any request for admittance to the rare book room on a need-to-know basis. Don't admit browsers. A person must have a specific inquiry or a special interest before being permitted to use the materials.

Use a locked door with a buzzer-type latch to protect the rare books area, and do not permit casual visitors to walk in and out of the room.

Don't let anyone (including staff) bring a coat, bag, or briefcase into the restricted area; instead, provide a checking area for these things.

If possible, always have a security person present and visible.

Adopt a system of marking all books with a library imprint. Also adopt a system of marking books that have been withdrawn from the collections; do not indicate withdrawal by removing or obliterating the imprint, but by using a special stamp with the date and the person's initials, certifying that this item has been formally withdrawn. Failure to do this makes it easier for a thief to sell stolen books, using a "withdrawn" stamp.

Report losses promptly, and invite local support through good public relations and news media interest. Awareness by the user public of a security problem may improve security.

Use discretion in hiring and managing after-hours workers, including janitors and security guards. Avoid giving these employees total freedom of movement in the library. Experience has shown that there will be an occasional problem person on the payroll, one who is capable of stealing and of even setting fires. Consider requiring a fidelity bond for each person, not only against recovery of a loss but also to take advantage of the credit investigation that the bonding company is likely to conduct on the person being bonded.

Since neither the turnstile method nor the electronic detection system fully protects rare books from theft, libraries have turned to other security strategies. The surveillance of rare book rooms by security forces and by library staff, for instance, has been found effective with and without CCTV. Likewise, more stringent and possessive measures and procedures, including restricted access to materials, are effective.

Intrusion Alarm Systems

While automatic systems for detecting fire and smoke are important for libraries, it is just as important to have an automatic intrusion alarm system to protect very valuable special collections. Libraries with very large properties may find it advantageous to consider purchasing a multiplex system, which can report various signals to a central station over a single pair of wires. Such a system can report intruders, fire, smoke, water, low water in a boiler, extremes of temperature or humidity, and other threatening situations.

Intrusion alarms also can be extended, when required by circumstances, to provide perimeter protection at a fence line or at a given distance from the library building. But more common are foils and traps on doors and windows, which detect the breaking of glass or the movement of a door, and devices that sense pressure on a floor covering or the presence of a person in a protected area. Some systems are subject to false indications when too finely tuned, however. Another device is a microphone that has a direct line to a central station, where a listener can hear sounds from the protected property, even the conversation of thieves and vandals.

Clearly, the intrusion protection system for the rare books and special collections has to be separate from any general or perimeter system. In a new facility, it should be a prime concern of the security consultant on the design and planning team. This is because it is likely that the rare book zone will be locked and vacant at times when the rest of the building is open for patrons or being serviced by custodians and maintenance men. Consider, for example, one of the nation's finest rare book facilities, which was built with a security system that was tested and found wanting by a student using a wire coat hanger.[13] This discovery led to the installation of a more reliable system at a far greater cost than would have been necessary if proper specifications had been written into the design at the time the building plans were still on the drawing board.

Book Theft Emergency Network

In 1982, the Antiquarian Booksellers Association of America (ABAA), in cooperation with four other organizations, put its security network into operation. The other organizations are (1) the Rare Books and Manuscripts Section, Association of College and Research Libraries, American Library Association, (2) the International League of Antiquarian Booksellers, (3) the Manuscript Society, and (4) the Society of American Archivists.

The ABAA security network has published an emergency routine for libraries to follow in notifying "everyone to whom the stolen material may be offered for sale, and everyone who can assist . . . in its capture and recovery."[14] For the theft of materials with a total value of over $5,000, libraries should first notify the ABAA security chairman and then the nearest office of the Federal Bureau of Investigation. For these materials and also for materials of lesser value, another eight steps are prescribed: notification of the library's attorney, insurer, and six agencies directly concerned with the problem of theft and the commercial traffic in stolen books. Full procedures are described in the system handbook, *Rare Books and Manuscript Thefts, a Security System for Librarians, Booksellers and Collectors.*

13. John W. Powell, "Architects, Consultants and Security Planning for New Libraries," *Library Security Newsletter* 1, no. 5 (Sept./Oct. 1975):6.

14. John H. Jenkins, *Rare Books and Manuscript Thefts, a Security System for Librarians, Booksellers and Collectors* (New York: Antiquarian Booksellers Association of America) 1982.

4 Fire Protection

The burning of a library is a national loss . . . there is generally a notion of perpetuity about collections of books: yet history sadly dispels the illusion. It seems, indeed, to be a fact that of all accumulated treasures books are the most liable to destruction. . . .[1]

Victor Hugo's browbeating of a revolutionary who burned a library requires sixty lines of couplets in *L'Année Terrible,* to which the revolutionary responds, "I don't know how to read." Hugo placed this passage under the title "À Qui la Faute?" with the implication that if the revolutionary had been educated, he would not have burned the library.[2] Persistent experience with arson in libraries should have us asking again, "Whose fault is it?"

Arson has become the leading source of library fire losses. The incidence of arson has risen to somewhere between 70 and 85 percent of all library fires, allowing for inadequate reporting of fires as well as other variables. For example, it is likely that abortive attempts to destroy libraries with fire are not reported at all. Even destructive fires are seldom considered newsworthy 300 miles distant from the afflicted library. Nonetheless, fires are bad news. Fires stopped by the prompt action of automatic systems are good news, but this news is not widely circulated, either.

Consider the following facts. The published information on library fires from 1950 to 1963 is meager.[3] Only 22 of the 61 fires of that period listed in a 1963 study were assigned a cause (table 1). Of these 22, only four were classed as incendiary, representing 18 percent of all reported library fires.

The data become more credible as more substantial information is made available in the following years. In the 1960–69 period, for instance, 36 destructive library fires were listed. Of these, 21 were assigned a cause, and nine were called incendiary, representing 47 percent of all library fires. In the following

---

1. Cornelius Walford, "The Destruction of Libraries by Fire Considered Practically and Historically, Proceedings of the 2nd Annual Meeting of the Library Association of the United Kingdom, Manchester, Sept. 23–25, 1879," reprinted in *Managing the Library Fire Risk,* 2nd ed. (Berkeley: Univ. of California, 1979), pp. 135–40.

2. E. A. Axon, "Victor Hugo on Books and Libraries," *Library Journal* 4 (June 1879):201.

3. Edward M. Johnson, ed., *Protecting the Library and Its Resources* (Chicago: American Library Association, 1963), pp. 225–30.

Table 1
Library Fires: Cause and Origin 1950–1981

	1950–59	1960–69	1970–79	1980–81
ARSON	4(18%)	9(47%)	43(78%)	17(85%)
Electrical	7	3	6	2
Heating system	3	2	5	1
Construction/maintenance	1	3	1	0
Exposure[a]	4	1	0	0
Smoking	2	0	0	0
Lightning	1	1	0	0
Total	22	19	55	20

Note: These figures represent only the 116 fires in which a "cause" or "origin" was determined. During the same years (1950–81), another 67 library fires occurred that were not assigned any cause. It is not unlikely that the incidence of arson in those 67 fires was very similar to that found in the cause-identified group.

[a]Exposure fires are any not originating in the library, but spreading to it from another building or another occupancy in the same building.

decade, 1970–79, 55 fires were identified. Of these, 43, or 78 percent, were called incendiary.

In 1980–81, there were 23 reported library fires, of which 17, or 85 percent, were listed as arson fires. Thus, a rising incidence of set fires is shown, beginning at 18 percent and rising to 47, then to 78, and then to 85 percent. However, it is not likely that the incidence was ever as low as 18 percent in the earlier years of the period 1950–81, since any number of the 67 unidentified fires may have been set fires.

The 1963 study was flawed in an important detail. Data collected by the National Fire Protection Association on *all building fires* showed smoking and matches to be the leading causes of fires, at 16 percent. Lacking other information, the study team extrapolated from this figure to conclude that the cause of library fires would follow the pattern established for all building fires. Yet only two of all the fires listed in the study were attributed directly to smoking.

The "smoking" statistic was unfortunately picked up by two eminent authorities on library design.[4] Although there is an obvious fire hazard related to smoking, the actual library fire experience is well under 1 percent from this cause, well behind electrical faults, heating system malfunctions, "hot work" in construction and maintenance, and lightning strikes. Incendiary (arson) fires set by burglars and vandals, and by children through book returns, are by far the most important and destructive. Fortunately, modern library design experts have recognized this in designing many fine library buildings in recent years, and such buildings now include vandal-resistant details and automatic fire detection and suppression systems.

4. Specifically Keyes D. Metcalf's *Planning Academic and Research Library Buildings* (New York: McGraw-Hill, 1965), 256, and Godfrey Thompson's *Planning and Design of Library Buildings,* 2nd ed. (London: Architectural Press, Ltd., 1973), p. 147.

Patterns of Arson

Three patterns are distinguishable in the occurrence of incendiary fires in libraries. The arsonist either pushes burning materials through the book drop or through a mail slot; or breaks into the building at night, looks for something to steal, then sets fires; or breaks a window or door glass and throws burning materials inside. Exceptions are fires set by employees in Cleveland and Baltimore libraries and the disaster of the Los Angeles Central Library of April 29, 1986, torched in the forenoon of a busy day.

Fire from Other Causes

The maintenance and construction operations of employees and outside contractors also have been responsible for destructive fires in libraries. For example, the great fire that destroyed the Birmingham Free Library in England was started by the blowtorch of a workman thawing out a pipe. As a result, some fine Shakespeare and Cervantes collections were lost, along with thousands of less important items. Another fire, stemming from blowtorch operations at the University of Montreal in 1962, destroyed the most complete endocrinology library ever assembled. Similarly, oxygen-fueled gas torches used without adequate safeguards in cutting and welding operations have started destructive fires in libraries at Wheaton College in Massachusetts, at the University of Texas in Austin, and at the National Film Archives near Washington, D.C. Other fires have been attributed to electrical faults, defective heating systems, and inadequate maintenance of equipment. All were obviously preventable.

Lightning has always taken its toll of libraries. In 188 A.D. several libraries in Rome burned during a violent storm in fires that followed lightning strikes. Great libraries also were destroyed in this way in France in 1300 and in Spain in 1674. Grambling State University lost about 50,000 volumes in 1962 in a fire that began when a bolt of lightning hit the library. In the fall of 1980, the Scottsville, Virginia, Branch Library suffered damages totalling $230,000 when a fire burned unobserved at night after a lightning strike. Dalhousie University in Halifax lost its law library and the entire fifth floor of the building in a fire that followed a lightning strike in August, 1985.

In view of these incidents, it is clear that a standard lightning protection system is a prudent investment, especially in the many areas known to be subject to electrical storms. The risk of lightning strikes varies widely across North America and elsewhere. Thunderstorms occur on an annual average of five days in coastal California, as often as 100 days in central Florida, and much more often in a few spots overseas. But the intensity of storms, not the frequency, is the important criterion of risk. Local experience and various environmental factors can help librarians determine the degree of predictable danger.[5]

The Los Angeles Central Library Fire

The burning of the Los Angeles Central Library on April 29, 1986, stands as the most costly library fire disaster in modern history. It demonstrated that a great

5. *Fire Protection Handbook,* 14th ed. (Quincy, Mass.: NFPA, 1976), pp. 56–63.

Following the Dalhousie University library fire in August, 1985, a Document Reprocessors crew prepares cases of wet books for the portable vacuum chamber in the background. *(Photograph courtesy of Eric Lundquist and Document Reprocessors.)*

library could be destroyed by fire in daylight in the middle of a large and highly organized city, and in spite of the best efforts of a mighty fire department working over a period of several hours. National Fire Protection Association investigators observed that the disaster could surely have been avoided by the action of an automatic sprinkler system.

It is surely ironic that the same conclusion was published following the Klein Law Library fire in Philadelphia in July, 1972. That fire also occurred on a busy day for the library, brought a massive response from the finest of fire departments, happened in the center of the city, and resulted in a multimillion dollar loss.

The Philadelphia disaster caused the insurance industry and risk managers everywhere to review their holdings in big libraries. McKeldin Library at the University of Maryland was recognized as having the highest concentration of property in Maryland, and vulnerable to a catastrophic fire loss. To make it an insurable risk required automatic sprinkler protection, and a complete system was duly designed and installed. Similar projects were undertaken at the University of California at Berkeley and at Stanford University. Large and important new libraries were designed with automatic systems. The Metropolitan Toronto and Hamilton (Ontario) central libraries were among these, and so were two very large libraries in Saudi Arabia. Likewise, James Madison Memorial Building of the Library of Congress was built with an impressive assortment of automatic systems suitable for protecting the nation's heritage of historic books and papers.

Furthermore, as fire protection engineers pointed out, the water disaster

Volunteers form a "bucket brigade" to rescue 3,000 books from the Klein Law Library fire. *(Photograph courtesy of Temple University.)*

that resulted from the Philadelphia fire (11,000 gallons per minute were poured into the building at one point) should be enough to convince anyone that automatic sprinklers could have prevented the flooding and immersion of that library's fine collections. One or two sprinkler heads would have opened when the fire was very small, and each head would have sprayed the fire with water at about 20 gallons per minute. The fire service officers, summoned by a waterflow alarm, would very likely have entered the library even before the staff knew about the fire; and they would have taken care to shut down the sprinkler branch line when the fire was out or when they took over the job of putting it out. The same scenario would have applied in Los Angeles.

Kathryn Linneman branch, St. Charles (Missouri) City-County Library is equipped with a complete automatic sprinkler system. *(Photograph courtesy of St. Charles City-County Library district.)*

Defenses against Fire

Fire-Safe Design and Construction

Protecting a library from fire was usually not a primary consideration in the design of library buildings until the latter half of the twentieth century. Yet as early as 1879, William Frederick Poole had expounded before a conference of the American Library Association the merits of building a compartmentalized library so as to confine a fire to a small portion of the library; he also suggested using protected iron and concrete for added fire resistance. In England at about the same time, automatic systems for extinguishing library fires were considered.

This was the era of the monumental library, following the example set by Henri Labrouste, architect of the Bibliothèque Nationale in Paris. Built during the years 1858–68, the Paris library had highly ornamented reading rooms with soaring ceilings, broad stairways, and a closed stack of purely utilitarian design. The stacks were "a small skyscraper within a building—a five-story framework of cast iron columns and wrought iron beams—a gigantic rack to house the shelving for 900,000 volumes. . . ."[6] This design caught the fancy of architects of large libraries, and hundreds of such libraries were built in Europe and North America between 1860 and 1930. It is remarkable that so few of these have been destroyed, so vulnerable was their construction. There were open stairways and open slots in the floors of stack levels, which would carry heat and smoke upward in the event of a fire; and the light metal of the supporting structure, quite unprotected from fire, would have buckled very early, dropping the collections into the fire below.

The Los Angeles Central Library was a classic example of the Labrouste design. The fire failed to cause the collapse of entire stack structures because of truly heroic measures taken by the firefighters and because the fire was set

6. Alvin Toffler, "Libraries," in *Bricks and Mortarboards* (New York: Educational Facilities Laboratories, Inc., 1964), p.73.

in the fifth or sixth tier of the seven-tier bookstacks. Although the collections in these tiers were reduced to black mud, the only total collapse was that of the seventh tier into the sixth in the hottest part of the fire, in the northeast stacks, where the fire originated.

New Designs   A revolt against the monumental design occurred in the 1940s, bringing in modular design—ceilings as low as eight feet plus a few inches; stacks in the form of bookshelves brought together with reading areas; and great flexibility for creating rooms and other areas for various library functions. During this period, air conditioning became common. Modifications to modular design emphasized the individual reader's need for semi-private study space, such as carrels and individual seating, and the traditional long wooden tables for eight or twelve people were removed. The atrium also came into its own.

This period of gradual change in library design was also a time of increasing acceptance of the need for better fire protection. Fire tests were made in Massachusetts and New York in the late 1950s to determine the need for automatic fire suppression in library stacks.[7] The tests produced mixed results. The Massachusetts tests proved that books on shelves could fuel a hot fire and that automatic sprinklers were effective in putting out such a fire. The Cornell University tests were made under different conditions to simulate a well-compartmented, fire-resistive situation, and the results indicated that sprinklers might not be needed. Fires in unprotected libraries in the period 1960–75 convinced insurors and librarians of the importance of automatic systems, both for detection and suppression of fires. The fire tests were then only of secondary interest.

Protection through Design   Libraries built since 1972 have generally had built-in fire protection, and quite a number of important older libraries had fire protection improvements made during these same years. The Library of Congress completed its new James Madison Memorial Building in 1979 and incorporated in it a formidable battery of fire defenses. These include early warning detection systems for fire and smoke, automatic suppression systems, automatic audible warning signals, a public address system, and smoke removal capability using the building's air handling system. Such a massive complex of systems is certainly appropriate for a building as large and important as the Madison Building, yet there are elements of fire protection design that are effective and within the reach of even the smallest of libraries.

Incendiary fires have destroyed more libraries than has any other type of fire by a factor of four to one. Book drop fires are common, and so are break-ins that are punctuated by set fires. Here are some simple ways of reducing the danger of these fires:

Safeguard the book return system. Replace it with a curbside book drop box, or strengthen it internally against any fire that might result from burning materials placed in it.
Strengthen rear windows and doors against casual vandalism.
Look for opportunities to subdivide the library with smoke-tight and fire

7. Edward M. Johnson, ed., *Protecting the Library and Its Resources* (Chicago: American Library Association, 1963), p. 208.

resistive construction. This is not as difficult as it might seem; even the vestibule at the front entrance can be made stronger and can be separated better from the next room.

Whenever a library is being planned, consider the interior finish and library furnishings and their potential for adding fuel to a fire. Bear in mind, for example, that noncombustible carpeting and draperies can be installed.

Other library fire protection information can be found in the chapter "Planning and Design."

Types of Automatic Fire Suppression Systems

Automatic extinguishment is universally accepted as the most effective defense against fire in buildings. The automatic fire suppression systems most often installed in libraries are water systems and Halon 1301 systems. When a new library is planned or improvements are wanted in an existing library, it is important to discuss the benefits of automatic fire suppression systems with architects and fire protection engineers. Here are brief descriptions of some possibilities:

Automatic Sprinklers   The extinguishing agent available everywhere at low cost is water, and the most cost-effective fire defense is an automatic sprinkler system. Yet in some quarters there is a lingering resistance on the part of librarians to accept sprinklers in bookstacks. They argue that the likelihood of fire occurring there is negligible, that water will somehow find its way out of the system when there is no fire, or that someone will find a way to sabotage the system as a witless prank or with malicious intent. Nevertheless, many large and important libraries now have bookstacks that are completely equipped with automatic sprinkler protection. In modern systems, movement of water in the pipes is signaled at once to a central station by a waterflow alarm. This brings a prompt response from the fire department and from any others who are notified by the central station, thus reducing the likelihood of any extensive damage occurring from an unwanted discharge, or from sprinkler action after a fire has been suppressed.

The design of a sprinkler system used to be dictated by schedules or formulas that sometimes provided more water through a larger pipe than was actually required by the nature of the property being protected. Modern fire protection engineering produces a custom-designed system that is better suited to the degree of fire hazard and that makes use of economical pipe layouts and pipes of reduced size. It is also sometimes possible, where the hazard is considered very light, to specify sprinkler heads with reduced orifice diameter that discharge less water. A system designed with such refinements is referred to as "hydraulically calculated."

The device that automatically sprays water on a fire is called a "sprinkler head." It has a cap or plug held securely in place by a heat-responsive alloy metal that has a low melting point and thus is designed to fail at a specific temperature and let the water out. It also has a deflector plate that is shaped and placed to distribute the water over a circular area of about 100 square feet. The amount of water discharged through the $1/2$-inch orifice varies with the water

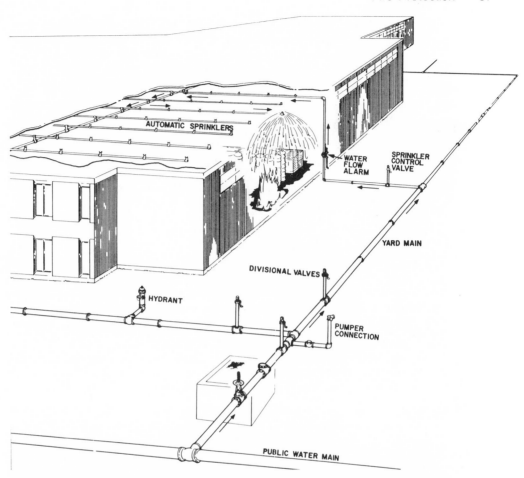

The workings of an automatic sprinkler system. This simplified diagram shows part of a sprinkler system and its water supply piping. When a fire actuates a sprinkler, water flows to it from public water mains as indicated by the arrows. The waterflow alarm operates even from the small amount of water used by a single sprinkler. The alarm on the building sounds, usually in a constantly attended area, or it transmits the alarm directly to the fire department, or to a central supervisory service which then calls the fire department. *(Drawing courtesy of the Factory Mutual System.)*

pressure and ranges from 15 to 20 gallons per minute. Sprinkler systems require a water pressure of 50 to 100 pounds per square inch (psi) to produce even the minimum pressure needed at points that are remote from the point of supply. Following are some specific types of sprinkler systems.

The *standard "wet pipe" automatic sprinkler system* is an arrangement of pipes below or above the ceiling, charged with water, and fitted at intervals with nozzles or sprinkler heads. Each head opens individually when it is heated to a critical temperature by a fire, and sprays water to control the fire. Most fires in sprinkler-protected buildings are subdued by the action of a single head or by that of a very few heads.

A *preaction system* is one in which water is withheld from the pipes until

Three different types of sprinklers: left, Flow Control flush mounted sprinkler head combines fast response technology with on-off action, opens quickly, shuts off when no longer needed, and reopens over a fire that rekindles *(Photograph courtesy of Central Sprinkler Corp.);* center, a standard horizontal sidewall sprinkler head for problem locations *(Photograph courtesy of Grinnell Fire Protection Systems Co., Inc.);* right, a cover plate used to conceal recessed sprinkler heads *(Photograph courtesy of Grinnell Fire Protection Systems Co., Inc.)*

fire or smoke is sensed by a detector; water then enters the pipes, and the system becomes essentially a "wet pipe" system and operated as such. Some libraries have selected this system because the hypothetical danger of a premature discharge from whatever cause is thought to be reduced. A further refinement of the preaction system is one in which the water is shut off, after a brief delay, when the temperature at the ceiling drops below 140°F. This is called a "recycling" system.

On-off (or stop-and-go) sprinkler heads are designed to act individually above a fire—opening to discharge water on a fire, and closing to stop the discharge when the fire is put out. This is a type of wet pipe system. One model has a deflector plate that spins freely and may have an advantage in producing a finer spray and better distribution. One development of the 1980s is the rapid-response sprinkler, which may have important implications for libraries. Originally conceived as a life safety device for promptly putting out fires in hospitals and residences, it may well be appropriate for other occupancies. A rapid-response sprinkler head will open early over a small fire and consequently will require less water to control the fire than does a standard head.

High-Expansion Foam   This extinguishing agent is produced by a fixed system, and the fire department also uses it with portable equipment for certain fire conditions. It has been used to protect document storage rooms in the British Public Record Office at Kew, near London. Since foam has the virtue of suppressing fire with very little water, it is possible that restoring materials after a fire fought with foam might be somewhat easier and cheaper than if the materials had been doused with water, as sometimes happens when a fire has to be fought with hose streams.

Halon 1301   Halon 1301 (CBrF$_3$, Bromotrifluoromethane) is the relatively innocuous, invisible gas now widely used to suppress fires in industries, museums, and rare book rooms. Valuable museum and library materials and fragile materials that might not survive being soaked with water are now being protected with Halon 1301 flooding systems. The action of the gas is virtually instantaneous in quenching a fire, and there are no residues whatsoever. Because it is not immediately harmful to persons in a room charged with the 5 or 6 percent of atmospheric concentration needed to defeat fire, Halon 1301 is the only agent approved by the National Fire Protection Association for totally flooding occupied space.

Because Halon 1301 is expensive, it is customary to protect against unwanted discharge of the system by cross-zoning detectors on separate circuits. Two well-separated sensors have to be triggered to release the agent and flood the area. An audible alarm is sounded, and a short delay is programmed into the system. In this way, the system can be aborted in the event that the problem is only a nuisance fire that can be readily managed with hand-held equipment.

The flooding system discharges all at once and with considerable velocity; therefore, fragile materials must not be placed close to discharge nozzles. Confinement of the gas is essential to its function by preventing dilution, so doors and windows of the protected area must be closed to insure effective action of the gas.

Total flooding systems using Halon 1301 in industrial settings have become progressively larger; there are now some as large as 30,000 pounds. An even more ambitious design calls for the protection of an entire multistory building with Halon 1301, making use of air handling ducts to selectively distribute the agent to the fire area. It requires relatively little hardware beyond what is needed for a conventional heating, ventilating, and air conditioning system, and promises to become competitive in cost with automatic sprinkler systems. This system may become common in buildings constructed in the twenty-first century.

In view of the extreme dependence on Halon 1301 suppression systems that exists in a large number of rare book rooms, it is appropriate to discuss the important characteristics of these systems. Here are some essential points to keep in mind when using or installing a Halon system:

> The protected area should be able to hold a 5 percent concentration of Halon 1301 for 10 minutes. Therefore, any contract bid for the installation of a Halon system should include the cost of a concentration test, using a less expensive agent (e.g., Halon 1211).
>
> The concentration test should be made before the system is accepted, using a three-point analyzer that samples the atmosphere at three levels: floor level, highest level needing protection, and at mid-level or about 5 feet off the floor. A very large room, however, may require a six-point test. The instrument must be field calibrated at the site.
>
> A graph of the test should show a 5 percent concentration at each level held for 10 minutes; an "average" of 5 percent for the three levels is a false result and should be refused. Moreover, by cutting a hole in the

aspirating tube at the floor level, an unscrupulous mechanic can show
a good concentration; this is not likely, but it has happened.

One manufacturer will check the plans and calculations of a local distributor, a desirable service in view of the values at stake.

The concentration test should also determine whether the action of dampers in ducts is satisfactory, whether magnetic door releases are satisfactory, whether nozzles are clear and properly adjusted, and whether
the required 5 percent concentration is achieved.

Another important benefit of the test for libraries is that it purges the pipes
and fittings of cutting oil and other contaminants that may lie within the system;
otherwise these might be spewed onto rare books when the Halon is eventually
discharged during an emergency.

Some regional codes require the installation of an exhaust system for removing smoke and fire gases from a Halon 1301-protected room following a fire. This is a questionable requirement, since most products
of combustion are toxic, and any amount of Halon 1301 used to extinguish a fire would rarely add measurably to the room's toxicity level.

One pound of Halon 1301 produces a 6 percent concentration in the air
in a space of 40 cubic feet. It is customary to figure a generous safety factor
into the system, but the concentration should be no more than 7 percent
maximum.

Several types of units are available for use with Halon 1301. *Modular* protection with Halon 1301 uses individual spheres or cylinders containing the agent in appropriate amounts, ranging from 10 to 196 pounds,
each receptacle being a self-contained system protecting its own area.
This is preferred when changes may be likely in a room or rooms, since
there will be no layout of pipes to remove and rebuild.

A *central storage* system may be needed for large spaces (in excess of 50,000
cubic feet). A *shared supply* system can protect several rooms. A selector valve
will release the agent from a single container and conserve the rest, or it will
release the entire supply, if needed, for a fire in the largest room. This system
requires a reserve supply, and the protected spaces must be separated by an
approved fire-resistive barrier. Another device is a *portable, self-contained system* (Firepac) that can be carried into a small room and plugged into any wall
receptacle, like any electrical appliance. It protects only 1,500 cubic feet but is
adequate for a vault or for a small room.

For preventing the unwanted discharge of the (costly) agent in a nuisance
fire (e.g., a fire in a wastebasket or in a copy machine), an "abort"
switch can be placed close to the control panel. However, there must
also be an on-off switch at the control panel.

When hot work, such as welding, must be done in the protected area, the
power may be disconnected temporarily, or a circuit breaker tripped,
to avoid setting off an alarm. One distributor offers a maintenance panel

Modular protection with Halon 1301. Containers range from 10 lbs. to 196 lbs. capacity. Each sphere is a self-contained suppression system. *(Photograph courtesy of Charles Sabah.)*

that leaves the system manually operational but temporarily removes the detection feature; it sounds an alarm every 30 minutes to remind the occupants that the system is not in full operation.

A photoelectric fire detector is the quickest device used for releasing the agent over a smoldering fire. Other releasing devices are ionization chamber smoke detectors and rate compensated rate-of-rise heat detectors. A service contract should be arranged for the periodic (semi-annual) inspection and cleaning of detectors. At this inspection, the weight of the agent should be checked; any containers that are not up to proper weight should be refilled without removing the containers. The date of the service call and the name of the inspector are then recorded on maintenance tags.

When a system is first purchased, the distributor should instruct the staff on all aspects of the system, including how to release the agent, how to abort the system, and how to use the manual control. The distributor also should respond to staff questions about the agent or the system.

Avoid making two separate contracts, one for the installation of a Halon system and another for the installation of a detection system to initiate the alarms and to discharge the agent. Sometimes neither the systems nor the contractors will work well together.

A multizone Halon system discharge control panel. *(Photograph courtesy of Fenwal.)*

The importance of the foregoing features becomes much clearer when a Halon 1301 system is seen in action. Therefore, the following description illustrates how this system typically operates.

In the event of a fire, an alarm is sounded when the first detector senses heat or smoke. At this point fans or blowers are shut down (in most systems), the magnetic door holders release doors to close, and the occupants of the room (if any) make a quick search for the source of the heat or smoke that was picked up by the detector. If another detector on the alternate circuit is activated, the system is primed to discharge in 15 seconds. The delay allows a further search for the fire and permits the occupants the option of aborting the system if there is no fire. A wastebasket fire or fire in a copy machine can be quenched with a hand-held extinguisher, an alternative that would save the very substantial expense of dumping the Halon 1301. The system does not discriminate between a smoking copy machine and a true fire emergency, and releases all the agent noisily and in a space of milliseconds.

Halon systems are used in explosion protection. Their action is so fast that an industrial process with a potential for explosion can be supervised by such a system. When the first spark or small flame of an explosion appears, it is sensed by a photoelectric detector and detonators release a blast of Halon; this inhibits the explosion which would otherwise have shattered the building and caused injuries or fatalities to workers nearby. The whole event from the first spark to complete suppression requires something less than 50 milliseconds, or one twentieth of a second. This kind of action would be welcome if a vandal dumped gasoline in a rare book room and ignited it, but it is too fast for most instances of fire emergency. The brief delay is important to sort out the facts and delay action of the system until you know that the emergency demands the commitment of your entire supply of Halon. Even with the delay built in, the protection of a sensitive area at night or at any time the library is closed is in good hands with a well-engineered Halon system.

A caveat expressed by fire protection engineers bears mentioning: Halon 1301 performs well under well-controlled conditions, but stringent requirements for good performance have to be observed. Doors and windows must be closed, and windows subject to being broken in an episode of vandalism would therefore be a point of weakness. So would a faulty ventilation system that might quickly dilute the required concentration of 4–6 percent. With these limitations in mind a dual system is sometimes to be considered, in which the primary Halon protection is reinforced by a sprinkler system.

If dampers are slow to close, a longer delay can be engineered into the system so that the concentration of the agent will not be diluted below the effective 5 percent level. In addition, the signal to the central station can be connected to the actual release rather than be activated by a sensor; this avoids false alarm runs by the fire department. Trouble alarms for a malfunction or a wiring problem go directly to the central station, of course.

The Halon 1301 build-up to the needed 5 percent air concentration takes just 10 seconds. If the ventilating system recirculates air only in the protected area, it can be left in operation; if not, it is shut down.

Carbon Dioxide   Carbon dioxide (CO_2) has been widely used in total flooding systems, primarily in industrial settings to put out surface fires in flammable liquids. It leaves no appreciable residues and has been used to protect at least one important repository for rare books. It is not approved, however, for use in occupied spaces because of the danger of suffocation. It has been used with success in the spot protection of the book return of a California library. A small CO_2 installation made at the suggestion of the architect paid off years later when vandals placed burning materials in the book drop, and the CO_2 discharged to suppress the fire.

Automatic Detection of Fire and Smoke

Another level of fire protection is automatic detection. A wide variety of devices and systems operate to sense the presence of flames, heat, or smoke, and send a warning signal. They have no suppression capability, and so any fire has to be put out by a fire department or emergency team summoned by the detection system. Nevertheless, it is likely that many libraries destroyed by fire in the past would have been saved through the timely message sent by such a system to a central station or fire department.

Automatic devices for sensing heat and/or smoke can perform various functions: (1) Sound an alarm in the building; (2) send an alarm to a fire department or to an alarm-monitoring station; (3) cause doors to close; (4) cause dampers to close; and (5) open valves to charge sprinkler pipes with water, etc.

Having a bell or other alarm sound on the premises is of no value unless people are present to recognize the signal and take action. Unfortunately, emergencies typically occur in the dead of night. Therefore, the alarm that brings help is likely one that transmits a signal directly to a monitoring station manned at all hours and where the signal can be interpreted and immediate action taken. This system is generally referred to as a central station system. Such a system when maintained by a university or another private entity to protect a number of buildings under one ownership is called a proprietary protective signaling system. Local alarm signals also can be maintained along with central station systems; this is a desirable feature in certain types of protection.

The principal devices for the automatic detection of fire include the following:

Ionization detectors, designed to sound an alarm when visible or invisible products of combustion enter a chamber in the device, interfering with the flow of electrical current through it.

Thermal rate-of-rise devices of many types, most of which confine air to a chamber with a very small opening for the escape of expanding air. When the heat of a fire causes a rapid expansion of air, greater than the capacity of the vent, the alarm is sounded. (A diaphragm moves, and electrical contacts are closed.) Frequently a fixed temperature alarm is used in the same system to provide secondary protection. Another form of rate-of-rise protection is a metallic tubing strung across ceilings in a building and hardly visible.

Photoelectric smoke detectors, which activate an alarm when smoke obscures a beam of light within the device.

Flame detectors. Several types are available, but these are probably more suitable for industrial applications. Libraries need the smoke- and heat-sensing features of other types.

Linear beam smoke detection, which has some advantages over other systems. An infrared beam is projected from a transmitter mounted on one wall to a receiver on the opposite wall as far away as 300 feet. It

Ionization smoke detector with adjustable sensitivity senses visible smoke or invisible products of combustion and sends an alarm. *(Photograph courtesy of Pyrotronics.)*

Linear beam infrared detector at University City (Missouri) Public Library. Transmitter and receiver face each other at opposite ends of the library; when smoke interrupts the beam, an alarm is sounded at a central station. Appropriate for atriums.

is said to indicate reliably any accumulation of light or dark smoke, and to be well suited to atrium protection.

Fixed temperature sensors of several kinds. These detectors are dependable, generally speaking, but are not as sensitive as early warning smoke detection devices. One system uses a continuous tape with two wires inside, which can be strung throughout a building.

Intrusion alarms. Because vandalism and arson have been increasingly the leading cause of destructive fires in libraries, it is important to consider intrusion alarms along with fire protection systems. Doors and windows can use traps against intrusion by burglars and vandals. Other alarm systems are also available, such as ultrasonic and infrared systems for detecting the movement of persons inside a closed library. Central station reporting of alarm signals is again important. Consultant services and the experience of others may be the best sources of information on these systems.

Multiplexing   One refinement in protective signaling systems is called "multiplexing," through which a variety of information can travel from the protected building to a central station (or another reporting point) over a single communications channel, e.g., a single pair of wires. This is done in one of two ways: by assigning different frequencies to various signals, or by "time division multiplexing," in which signals are identifiable by their position in relation to other signals in a continuous, very rapid transmission. For example, fire, smoke, water, sprinkler action, and excessive humidity would all be reported over one pair of wires in multiplexing.

Although costs such as installation and maintenance should be reduced in multiplexing, it is not necessarily cost-effective for even a large library. It is of maximum value in extremely large buildings or in groups of buildings that require a single reporting system for alarms; it is also of value when information is required to be sent to various locations for action, rather than to a central station. A careful engineering study of a library's signaling protection requirements can determine whether or not multiplexing is desirable. Because the science of communications is constantly advancing, it is likely that new developments appropriate to the protection of libraries will appear from time to time.

The Alarm System Contract   For most large libraries, with the possible exception of large academic libraries, alarm systems are contracted out to a security organization with central station capability. This contract should be placed with care, and only after a careful check is made of the contractor's experience and local reputation. The contractor should agree to provide such services as complete regular inspections of the system, recordkeeping on inspections made, and maintenance and alarm calls. Any parts and equipment needing replacement during normal use of the system should be furnished free of charge. The automatic standby battery system that provides auxiliary power during a failure of the regular power supply also should be checked as part of the maintenance schedule. The contractor's primary duty, of course, is to receive any emergency signals the system may communicate and to take immediate action on them. The contractor also should assist any emergency response agency on the scene by resetting the alarms and securing the premises.

Before an alarm system is purchased, it is important to check out the system's hardware and to inquire of other libraries about their experience. The label or listing of a product by a nationally recognized testing laboratory is almost universally seen as a sufficient warranty of excellence. But it is good to bear in mind that the label or the listing applies usually only to the unit tested, not to the entire system.

Inquiries into specific products might turn up such comments as the following: The manual alarm stations have operated spontaneously because the breakglass rod was under too much tension; others required so much force to operate that they were pulled out of the wall when the alarm was sounded. . . . Absolutely unworkable smoke detectors have been listed. Clearly, it is useful to learn from colleagues in other local libraries and from local fire protection engineers what their actual experience with such systems and devices has been.

Night Security Personnel   It is sometimes suggested that most of the emergencies that are reportable through an automatic signaling system might well be reported by a janitor or night security personnel. This is not likely. Security people, even the best, cannot approximate the ubiquity and sensitivity of a multifunction alarm system. It is a matter of record that they have inadvertently been responsible for fires and other unfortunate events. Janitors cannot do their work and be held responsible also for fire detection; one costly fire in an academic library burned undetected for some time while janitors carried out their proper duties in other rooms in the building.

Failures of Automatic Systems   The importance of intelligent design, maintenance, and periodic testing of automatic systems cannot be overstressed. Following are some examples of library fire and water casualties that occurred because of errors in design or maintenance:

A sprinkler head discharged in a building at night because it had been installed directly opposite a space heater.

A college library burned in the night; the fire department came to the campus but could not readily locate the fire, because a contractor had failed to connect the library's alarm circuit to the annunciator panel that pinpoints the origin of the alarm signal. The delay was costly.

A preaction system was being drained; water splashed out of an open drain unobserved and found its way downstairs into the books.

A sprinkler head with a low-temperature melting point was installed at the top of a light well where it got very hot; the head responded and poured water on carpeting and furnishings.

Fire that burned out a library went undetected for some time because the alarm circuits were being tested, and fire signals were misinterpreted as test signals.

A college library was protected in some areas with automatic sprinklers and in others with "products of combustion" detectors, but a large reference room was unaccountably left out of the detection system. A costly fire originated there and burned for some time before smoke was carried through ducts to a protected room where it activated a sensor and sounded the alarm.

Thieves entered the rare book room of a college library through an emergency exit door leading to a stairway; the intrusion alarm did not operate. It had been tested in every way except by opening the door. The thieves made off with three rare books from a display case.

A school library was destroyed when thieves broke in and set fires as they left. A sonic intrusion alarm system protected the library, but it had been taken out of service by a staff member who anticipated false alarms being caused by a noisy party in the neighborhood.

Such incidents as these illustrate the importance of regularly maintaining and testing automatic fire detection and suppression systems so that they will function properly in an emergency. Moreover, they should be central station systems and electrically supervised to signal faults in the system itself. Electrical supervision is also essential for automatic sprinkler systems, particularly to report an unauthorized closing of the valves that supply water to the system. And once installed, automatic systems need to be kept in good operating condition to provide the protection intended.

Protecting Book Returns   Returning to Victor Hugo's question, "À qui la faute?" relative to arson and libraries, we cannot today place the blame on ignorance or inability to read on the part of the arsonists. If we know that fire comes in through book drops, for instance, and we do nothing about it, who is at fault? Indeed, book returns and back doors are the places where child arsonists usually strike. Many libraries have met the threat head on with improved facilities. For example, Diablo Valley College in California strengthened its book return with a stainless steel receiving box that has a spring-loaded platform inside to accept the books. The first books that are deposited do not immediately fall to the bottom of the box. Instead, the platform moves down gradually as more books are deposited, saving wear and tear on books.

In Clayton, Missouri, the Mid-County Library offers three points for the separate deposit of books, tapes, and records. Other libraries have placed book returns outside and permanently closed the openings into the library.

Kings Park Library in Burke, Virginia, has a receiving room for the book return that is admirably separated from the library proper and that once confined an incendiary fire. The Kathryn Linneman Branch Library in St. Charles, Missouri, has an automatic sprinkler head in the receiving room for the book drop. Another type of protection is an automatic suppression unit within the book return itself. At a library in Palos Verdes, California, a CO_2 device installed in the receiving area controlled a fire set by an arsonist.

Although "spot protection" of this type is not given high marks by fire protection engineers, who generally recommend protecting the entire building, it

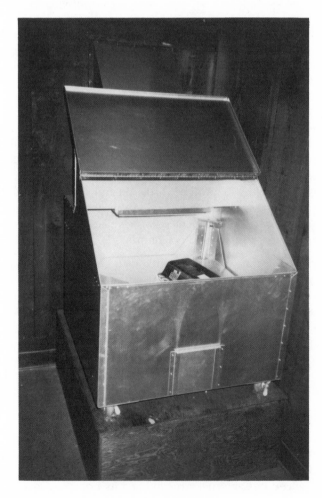

The Diablo Valley College Library improved its book return with a stainless steel-enclosed chute and receiving bin, fitted with a spring-loaded floor that lowers as more books are placed on it.

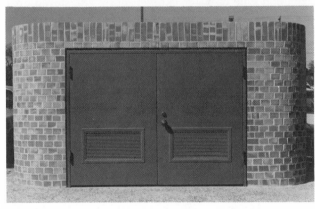

Book drop at curb, front and back views: Elizabeth Coates Maddux Library, Trinity University. *(Photographs courtesy of Craig S. Likness.)*

can be justified on the strength of libraries' experience with such fires. A Halon 2402 device and various other small extinguisher units that are very limited in capacity may indeed have a place in book returns. Moreover, a single automatic sprinkler head, especially one with on-off action, piped from any reliable water line would have prevented most of the devastating book return fires that have occurred. The National Fire Protection Association already approves similar spot protection for special fire hazard areas in schools.

First-Aid Fire Protection (Extinguishers)

Most local fire codes require that one or more portable fire extinguishers be placed in any building that is subject to the code. All portable extinguishers contain a pressurized substance that can be expelled on an incipient fire from a distance of 10 to 50 feet. The time of discharge is sometimes short, under 10 seconds for some small units. If the fire is still quite small, a person who uses the appropriate extinguisher with skill can probably put it out. The types of extinguishers particularly suited to use in libraries are listed here:

> Pressurized water, best for use on paper and wood fires, but not to be used on electrical equipment or on flammable liquids.
> Halon 1301 or Halon 1211; both are appropriate indoors for use on any fire.
> Dry chemical; usable on any fire, but leaves a powdery residue.
> Carbon dioxide (CO_2); suitable for electrical and flammable liquid fires, leaves no residues, but is not as good as other substances on wood and paper fires.

However, fire defense with hand-held extinguishers has several limitations. People are usually untrained in their use and in an emergency don't know where the extinguishers are. Moreover, fire frequently strikes when nobody is around to use an extinguisher. If they are able to take action when fire is discovered, they are liable to use one, two, three, or more extinguishers to try to put it out before sending the alarm to the fire department; the delay can be disastrous. First the alarm should be sent, then the extinguishers can be put to use.

It may be instructive to look more closely at some of the more common extinguishers. The most common type of water extinguisher is the stored pressure type. It has a chamber of pressurized air and a valve like that found on an automobile tire. It is usually charged at 90 to 120 pounds, enough to expel $3^{1}/_{2}$ gallons of water from 35 to 40 feet horizontally for about 55 seconds, either continuously or intermittently. It may have a simple ring and pin device to prevent accidental discharge while it is being carried. To put water on the fire, it is important to remove the pin by pulling on the ring. It is also good to replace any metal pin with a commercially available frangible pin. Even the bungling user, who invariably fails to remove the pin, will be able to use the device because the pin will shear when the handle is squeezed. If the extinguisher lacks the frangible pin, it is common in a fire emergency for excited and untrained people to bend the metal handle out of shape because they have not removed the pin; this makes the extinguisher useless.

One other type of water extinguisher is the pump tank, which holds $2^{1}/_{2}$ to 5 gallons of water, weighs up to 50 pounds, has to be carried to the scene of a fire, and has to be pumped vigorously to be useful. A back pack model is widely used in fighting fire in the woods and open country.

Obsolete water types are soda-acid and foam extinguishers, which have not been produced since 1969. They have an inherent explosion hazard as they grow older and if they are not well maintained; injuries and deaths have been recorded when they are suddenly operated in an emergency. Furthermore, they cannot be turned off, once activated, and the contents are corrosive. These old types should be discarded. Any extinguisher that has to be inverted is obsolete, as is any carbon tetrachloride or other vaporizing liquid unit. Pint-sized or beer-can type extinguishers are so limited in capability that they cannot be recommended.

On the other hand, Halon 1301 extinguishers are given a good rating by the National Fire Protection Association and have characteristics appropriate to any library use. Another Freon, Halon 1211, is somewhat cheaper than Halon 1301 and is accepted for use in hand-held units; however, it is also somewhat more toxic than Halon 1301. Still another available extinguisher is charged with a blend of Halon 1211 and Halon 1301, and is said to be highly effective.

For work areas, receiving rooms, shipping rooms, storage areas, and maintenance shops, a suitable length of garden hose may be kept coiled and attached permanently to a water line. This is an excellent weapon against fires. It is something familiar to everyone, is easily managed, and has a virtually inexhaustible supply of extinguishing agent, unlike a portable extinguisher. With the right kind of nozzle, it is capable of emitting a fine spray or a solid stream, as needed.

A large-diameter fire hose, sometimes stored in cabinets in large buildings and attached to standpipe risers, is not well suited for use by building personnel. It should be left for the fire department; however, they usually bring their own hose, knowing that what is stored in cabinets is frequently unusable. Water pressure in a large diameter hose makes it very dangerous for any untrained person to try to handle it.

Emergency Routine   The standard fire emergency routine is approximately as follows. When you discover a fire:

Warn others in the immediate vicinity and in the building.
Send the alarm through a manual alarm-sending station or by telephone to the fire department.
Confine the fire by closing doors and windows, and shut down the air handling system to prevent circulating fire gases and smoke throughout the building.
Take any fire-fighting action that does not expose you or others to injury.
Take any preplanned action that will protect valuable property and vital records (e.g., closing a fire door at the entrance to the rare book room).

Developing a routine like this will help avoid a delay in sending the alarm.

Chart 1 shows how an incipient fire can be controlled manually by one person when its area is quite small, and how the chance for putting it out evaporates as the minutes go by and the fire spreads. One person using an extinguisher skillfully on a small fire of 4 feet by 5 feet (20 sq. ft.) has a probability of success of 95 percent in suppressing the fire. If the fire is twice as large (40 sq. ft.), the chance of success is only 20 percent. As the fire spreads, the chance of success quickly drops to zero. A similar curve of diminishing opportunity faces the trained employee fire brigade or the professional fire department.[8]

Fire Prevention

Fire prevention is the term given to activities that are intended to reduce the possibility of fire. A fire prevention program consists of a purposeful series of posters, pamphlets, printed instructions, training sessions, and inspection routines. Fire prevention is a part of the larger entity called fire protection. A building with good fire protection should survive a fire. However, one that lacks

8. Rex Wilson, *Measurement of Building Firesafety* (Wellesley Hills, Mass.: FIREPRO, Inc.).

Chart 1. Extinguishing Capability vs. Size of Flame Area
Success Rate of Manual Extinguishment

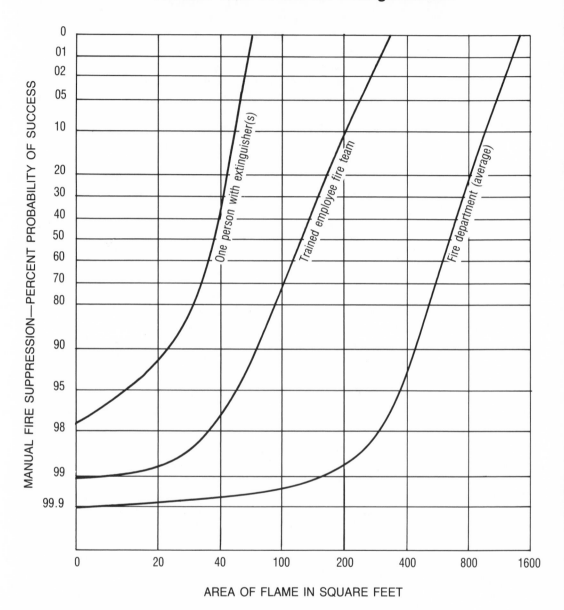

Adapted from the workbook *Measurement of Building Firesafety. Courtesy of Rex Wilson,*
FIREPRO, Inc., Wellesley Hills, Massachusetts.

essential fire protection elements could be destroyed in a fire in spite of a great fire prevention program.

A fire prevention program for a large library should include the following components:

Staff instruction in the emergency routine that should be followed when a fire is discovered.

Staff training and instruction in how to use portable fire extinguishers.

Regular fire inspections by an outside fire marshal and by a staff person trained for this function.

Attention by the fire marshal to special hazards that might be present during an event requiring combustible construction or decorations.

Special attention to any jobs performed by maintenance workers or outside contractors in which there is a possible fire hazard (e.g., welding and cutting operations, use of flammable solvents and like materials).

Staff should also conduct a closing time inspection each day. Following are some suggestions on what to watch for during this inspection:

Waste paper and other combustible trash should be placed in a metal can with a tight-fitting lid; do not use paper bags or plastic or paper containers for trash.

Trash should be removed from the building daily, if possible. If this is not possible, trash should be placed in a room designed to contain fire or in one that has an automatic fire suppression system.

Check for coffeemakers or other electrical devices left energized at the end of the day; a red pilot light is useful in showing when the device is energized.

Fire doors and smoke barrier doors should be closed.

Check for smoking materials carelessly left in the wrong place or in the wrong receptacle.

Check for door and window security and for people who should have left the library at closing time.

Also be sure to watch for the following fire hazard items:

Are *No Smoking* rules enforced effectively? Is there a *Smoking Permitted* arrangement for compulsive smokers? Are safe ashtrays and receptacles provided?

Are draperies noncombustible? Is carpeting noncombustible or slow burning?

Do any large exhibits or decorations present a fire hazard? If a Christmas tree is displayed, be aware of the danger and tragic history of tree fires; consult the local fire department.

Are maintenance supplies and tools, oily mops, cleaning fluids, paints, thinners, etc., stored in fire resistant areas or in metal cabinets approved for this purpose? Keep only a minimum quantity of these items on hand, preferably stored in a room designed to contain fire or in a room that has an automatic fire suppression system.

Has everyone been adequately instructed in fire emergency procedures?

Are instructions posted? Is the telephone number of the fire department prominently displayed?

Is all heating equipment in good condition, including flues?

Is steam boiler inspection and maintenance performed at proper intervals? Is adequate makeup air provided?

Is the air conditioning system regularly serviced?

Are filters clean in the air handling system?

Is there makeshift wiring (especially in maintenance areas, nailed in place, or draped over nails) that should be replaced with approved wiring?

Are there any electrical extension cords longer than six feet? Are any cords run under carpeting, or are cords in any other places where they can be damaged and start a fire?

Are fire doors and smoke barrier doors properly maintained? Are they properly closed at closing time?

If there is a fire, does the fire department have access to the building without having to break down a door?

Contract Operations Contractors who build a new library or make alterations in an existing library frequently introduce acute fire hazards. Welding and cutting operations, copper pipe brazing, floor covering installation, painting, and various other operations sharply increase the risk of fire. When alterations or repairs involve portable welding equipment or open flame devices of any kind, it is important to take stringent measures to control the fire hazard. A permit procedure is widely used in industry, outlining specific fire prevention measures, and any library would be well advised to demand this kind of routine in welding, cutting, or other "hot work." As with any repair or alteration work involving the presence of workmen or mechanics, especially those hired by an outside contractor, it is advisable to have the job surveyed in advance by the proper fire prevention officer or fire marshal. While the work is in progress, a person whose sole concern is the prevention of fire should survey the work. When a new building is under construction, water supplies that are adequate for construction operations may be quite inadequate for fire department operations. Where this is true, a temporary standpipe and hose can be installed, or even a temporary automatic sprinkler system can be used. Emergency access for fire apparatus should also be considered. The fire department should be invited to make recommendations on these points and to make inspections of the job in progress.

Fire Protection/Questions and Answers

If Halon 1301 is an ideal extinguishing agent for use around books, why not protect the whole library with it?
The cost of using this agent to protect any very large area would be prohibitive for most libraries; there are also technical problems to overcome.

Is it possible to sabotage automatic sprinkler systems?
Possible, yes, but instances of this have been very rare. When a system is electrically supervised, any tampering with the valves or any movement of water in

the pipes sends a signal to the central station, setting up an emergency response by the fire department and other agencies.

Can some areas of a building be protected by automatic systems without protecting the entire building?
It is possible, but experience has shown that this is liable to be a false economy; fires tend to strike in unprotected areas. One possible exception would be book returns, which have such a notorious arson record that spot protection for the receiving area might be worthwhile.

Don't sprinkler heads make a room ugly?
Not really; they can even be quite difficult to see in some places, as in the lofty ceiling of the circulation room of Doe Library at Berkeley, California, where they are totally lost in the ornamentation. They can also be installed above the ceiling, concealed by a decorative disc that falls away when the heat at the ceiling reaches a critical temperature.

What effect do automatic systems have on insurance costs?
Discounts are considerable. They can sometimes amortize the original cost of the system over a period of a few years.

Does a standard wet pipe system sprinkler head continue putting out water until a valve is closed in the supply line?
Yes, but stoppers are available that can be put into the sprinkler fitting to stop the water when it is no longer needed. This restores the system at once; the spent head can be replaced later. A wedge of soft wood also can be shaped for this purpose by a competent mechanic.

Our new central library will have a large area of compact storage in the basement. Is there any special fire protection problem in this installation?
Yes. Studies were conducted in 1978 for the General Services Administration by Factory Mutual Research Corporation. They found that the fire loading in these systems is greater by far than in conventional shelving.[9] Any fire would have to be controlled early to prevent a very hot and very stubborn problem for a fire department. Automatic sprinkler protection is indicated, as well as the counsel of a fire protection engineer.

What about storage of motion picture film?
There are two kinds of film. Modern film has a cellulose acetate base, which has burning characteristics similar to those of paper; fire protection for this is described in NFPA 232, *Protection of Records*. Nitrate film, produced from 1900 to 1951, has a base of cellulose nitrate, or nitrocellulose. It is dangerous to store without compliance with numerous and stringent restrictions. These are set forth in NFPA 40, *Standard for the Storage and Handling of Cellulose Nitrate Motion*

9. Peter J. Chicarello, J. M. Troup, and R. K. Dean, *Fire Tests in Mobile Storage Systems for Archival Storage,* Technical Report No. J.I. 3A3N4.RR (Norwood, Mass.: Factory Mutual Research, June, 1978).

Picture Film. Requirements include automatic sprinklers, fire resistive construction, limited quantity, and explosion venting of storage spaces. Historic and unique films have been lost in fires in film archives for lack of adequate safeguards.

Is the installation of a sprinkler system something that any licensed plumber can handle?

No indeed; it is most important to have a contractor who is certified for sprinkler installations. Manufacturers of sprinkler fittings and equipment can provide the library with a sample contract complete with performance specifications that should screen out an incompetent contractor.

Did the Los Angeles disaster yield any new information about fire protection for libraries?

No. However, we can hope that it will convince library professionals about the real danger of incendiary fire and the importance of good compartmentation and automatic suppression systems.

Do sprinklers discharge water when there is a false alarm?

No. When a hot fire raises the temperature above the level for the sprinkler head closest to the fire, the head opens and showers the fire. The fire department is alerted at the same time through a waterflow alarm.

Are only the big, new libraries installing sprinkler systems?

No, the Hollywood Branch of the Los Angeles Public Library, burned out in an incendiary fire in 1982, was rededicated in June, 1986, with a complete automatic sprinkler system. Other libraries of moderate size so protected include those of Gaithersburg and Cockeysville in Maryland, Linneman Branch in St. Charles, Missouri, and Fremont, California, Main Library. Most important academic libraries have installed automatic protection of one sort or another.

5 Water Damage: Protection and Recovery

We need not consider the damage from water thrown on books to save them from burning as being beyond remedy. Even when books escape from a fire (as is often the case) in a parboiled condition, it is still only a question of patient but skillful treatment.[1]

The most common calamities for libraries are surely water incidents. Of these, natural disasters of great violence are the most damaging; these include floods, hurricanes, and tornadoes. The great flood at Florence in 1966 may have been the worst water disaster in modern history. Fine old books were soaked in foul water, mud, and fuel oil; abraded by gravel; and battered by streams of water under great pressure. The vast restoration program that ensued enabled conservation professionals to refine the known techniques of salvaging and repairing damaged books and works of art while working under the most difficult conditions imaginable. The lessons of the Florence experience and of two major U.S. disasters in 1972 and 1973 are reflected in a scholarly and indispensable handbook by Peter Waters called *Procedures for Salvage of Water-Damaged Library Materials.*[2]

A study published in 1963 reported that 153 libraries experienced a total of 257 incidents of losses due to water damage, of which only a few were related to fires and fire department operations. The rest resulted from breaks in water and steam lines, construction operations, seepage, rainstorms, leaking roofs, faulty drains and sewers, and the like.[3] In more recent history, water used in air handling systems has occasionally found its way into the library.

1. Cornelius Walford, "Destruction of Libraries from Fire Considered Practically and Historically," *Transactions and Proceedings of the Second Annual Meeting of the Library Association of the United Kingdom* (London, 1880).

2. Peter Waters, *Procedures for Salvage of Water-Damaged Library Materials* (Washington, D.C.: Library of Congress, 1975).

3. Edward M. Johnson, ed., *Protecting the Library and Its Resources* (Chicago: American Library Association, 1963), pp. 18–19.

Water Damage Prevention

Extensive experience with water incidents in libraries has enabled professionals concerned with preservation to make recommendations not only for disaster preparedness but also for preventing flooding and water disasters. Since fires so often produce water damage, some of the points that follow relate to fire hazards, and others strictly concern water disaster prevention:

Know the water hazards of the region, such as the flooding history of the past century; the potential for a dam break in the area; and the region's experience with electrical storms, snow, landslides, tornadoes, and hurricanes. Also know the level of the water table.

Perform surveys aimed specifically at preventing fire-and-water incidents.

Set up a program for the maintenance of fan and blower motors, such as those found in air handling systems.

Know the water damage potential of water mains, automatic sprinklers, water pipes, roof drains, sewer lines, floor drains, toilets, drinking fountains, and rooftop air conditioning apparatus.

Know the drainage patterns that exist both inside and outside the building; have an efficient sump pump and a reserve pump for emergency situations.

Check for low shelves and books stored on the floor or close to it; these are vulnerable to any water incident, especially in a basement room.

Consider earthquakes, wherever appropriate: Is shelving strongly braced at the top and at floor level? Are shelves containing valuable items sloped to prevent spilling? Are water pipes properly supported with sway bracing? Are records and recording tapes restrained?

Automatic Water Warning Systems

One form of protection against water incidents that should be more widely used is a 24-hour automatic warning system that sends a signal notifying a central station of the presence of unwanted water so that an emergency crew can be summoned. Such an alarm sometimes uses a cellulose sponge, like that found in most households. The rapid expansion of the sponge, when it picks up water, closes an electrical circuit and sends a signal.

Another water detection system, called Early Warning Aid, was developed in Sweden and has the endorsement of the Försäkringsbolagens Service AB, a national testing agency. It not only transmits its own alarms for water, humidity, and temperature extremes, but can also carry signals originating in intrusion detection and fire detection devices. Yet another system, Raychem TraceTek® 100, has the special capability of not only sensing the water but reporting its location precisely. It employs a continuous polymer sensing cable and an electronic locator module. The cable contains a continuity wire, a signal return wire, and two sensor wires, polymer coated to resist corrosion. When water is present, the module sounds an alarm and shows in a digital display how many feet or meters away the water is from the end of the cable. This system is also listed by Underwriters Laboratories.

The local fire department should be consulted about these matters, as well

Earthquake protection at University of California, Santa Barbara. Photos on the left and lower right show retainer tapes for phonograph records; upper right photo shows overhead bracing to prevent shelves from toppling. *(Photographs courtesy of Larry Parson.)*

as about aspects of fire prevention. They should be familiar with the library's fire and water detection and suppression systems, the location of its special collections, and areas where the use of salvage covers would be especially beneficial in the event of a fire. A fire officer also should participate in the library's disaster planning. The fire department should also be invited to make company inspections of the building so as to familiarize firefighters with the layout of the rooms.

Salvaging Wet Books

Freeze-drying and vacuum-drying techniques for salvaging wet books came into being in the late 1960s. It was logical that processes used so widely for desiccating food products would eventually be put to use for salvaging wet library materials. When the regional library in Gothab, Greenland, burned in February, 1968, books soaked by water from fire hoses froze at once into icy clumps and were shipped in this condition to Denmark for restoration. Certain items of historical interest were too delicate for ordinary air drying; therefore, these were placed in heated vacuum chambers for 36 hours or longer. As the vacuum was gradually reduced, the ice was sublimated into vapor, bypassing the water stage and leaving the papers in good condition. Even handwritten ink inscriptions did not run. The process was entirely successful. This was the first of many successful vacuum freeze-drying book salvage operations.

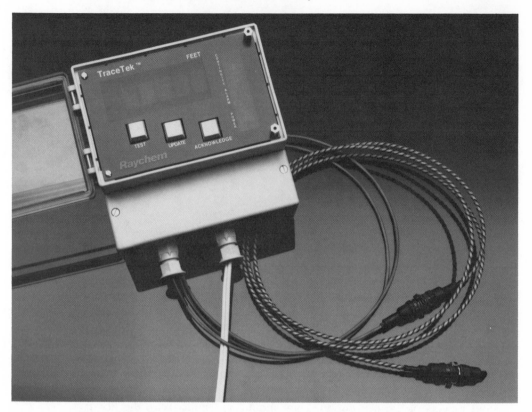

Raychem's TraceTek® 100 System detects the presence of any unwanted water and reports precisely where it is in the building. *(Photograph courtesy of Raychem Corporation.)*

In subsequent years, two very large fire disasters in the United States focused attention on the salvage of large water-damaged collections. These were the July, 1972, fire in the Klein Law Library of Temple University in Philadelphia, and the fire one year later at the National Military Records Center in Overland, Missouri. The two recovery operations differed in one important detail: the Philadelphia library had fine books to be restored, while the Records Center needed only readable copy to reconstruct their files.

The Philadelphia library was handicapped by the absence of a disaster plan for coping with an overwhelming fire and water emergency. There were no duplicate records, for example, to help determine what was missing. Books were treated to retard mold, then wrapped in paper and frozen before being taken to General Electric facilities at Valley Forge to undergo the vacuum chamber procedure. Records Center files, on the other hand, went directly to vacuum chambers and were successfully dried without ever being frozen, even some that had been wet for four months and had become moldy. Processing was done at McDonnell Douglas in St. Louis and at a NASA installation in Ohio.

The deep freezing of wet books at $-20°F$ ($-29°C$) or colder is recommended by conservators as an important first step in the restoration of wet books and other library materials. This stabilizes damage from water, inhibits mold, and defers indefinitely the need for other processes. It also has a beneficial effect on coated papers, which otherwise tend to become glued together.

The University of Toronto may have been the first to respond to a major fire and water emergency by making use of a disaster plan set up for their libraries. When a night fire destroyed the Sir Sandford Fleming Building in February, 1978, a "Disaster Contingency Plan," worked out in 1976, was activated to salvage collections from the engineering library. University staff members carried out their preassigned duties, and commercial establishments previously enlisted for emergency aid came through with urgently needed services and supplies. Out of 80,000 items, 17,000 were destroyed as not worth repairing; the rest were repaired and returned to the shelves. Of these, 500 rare or hard-to-replace books went to a military vacuum chamber for drying.

Stanford University suffered a major water incident late in 1978 when a water main outside a new library building failed during the night, and water entered the library through pipe openings in the basement wall. More than 50,000 books were soaked. They were restored during the months that followed, after being dried in a very large vacuum chamber modified for the purpose.

Still another chapter in the history of wet book restoration was written in

Lockheed Missiles & Space Co. of Sunnyvale, California, STARS vacuum chamber converted for vacuum freeze-drying wet books following the Stanford Meyer Library flood of November 4, 1978. Books are arranged by size, spines against the heated back of the rack, about 5,000 books at a time. *(Photograph courtesy of the Lockheed Missiles & Space Co., Inc.)*

1980 with a portable vacuum chamber acquired by a San Francisco entrepreneur for salvaging books and manuscripts.[4] When an incendiary fire resulted in the waterlogging of thousands of documents in the New Jersey state archives, a call was issued for a salvage organization that could process the wet papers on the site. The California firm was able to load its 6,000 pounds of equipment on a 747 aircraft and take it to New Jersey.

The location of available freezer and vacuum chamber facilities should be noted in every library's disaster plan. Generally speaking, such facilities can be found at plants that are operated by the major aerospace contractors. Food industry warehouses are also likely resources. Smaller units can be found on university campuses; however, these are not usually adapted for processing wet books. Information on restoration facilities also can be obtained from other libraries and from the Preservation Office at the Library of Congress.

The conventional air drying of books and papers is by no means obsolete. When materials are lightly wet (not submerged), and when the number of items to be treated is well within the capacity of the available work force, traditional methods are practicable. But if coated papers are soaked, as well as large numbers of fine and rare books, it is certainly worth the extra effort and expense required to freeze the materials and to call upon the best professionals that are available to help with the restoration.

Stanford's Water Disaster: A Case History

The Stanford University water casualty of November 4, 1978, came twelve years to the day after the Florence flood disaster. Because it is typical of library water accidents in several ways, and because it demanded emergency action to save a very large number of books, it is useful to review in brief what happened from start to finish.[5]

Shortly before 3 A.M., a deteriorated 8-inch water main failed underground outside Stanford's Meyer Library, and water poured into the basement stacks through two holes that had been drilled for pipes. The drop in water pressure sounded an alarm, and within 20 minutes the water was shut off. The area affected had two tiers of metal shelving containing about 400,000 volumes, and more than 50,000 of these items became wet to one degree or another.

In accordance with disaster guidelines formulated nearly a year earlier, the library mobilized an emergency force of workers, and a coordinator was appointed. Peter Waters' *Procedures* pamphlet was distributed and studied. Unfortunately, the freezer company named in the disaster plan could not accommodate the 50,000 books, but a very large plant 25 miles away was located and used instead. A local dairy provided milk crates for transporting the books, and trucks were loaned by several local companies.

The air handling system was adjusted to provide the maximum volume of cool, fresh air to reduce humidity, and in a few hours the humidity level dropped to below 50 percent. A decision was then made to freeze the wet books and

---

4. Eric Lundquist, doing business as Document Reprocessors.

5. Sally A. Buchanan and Philip D. Leighton, *The Stanford-Lockheed Meyer Library Flood Report* (Stanford, Calif.: Stanford University Libraries, 1980).

materials promptly, and a deadline of 48 hours was set for accomplishing this task. Consequently, all the books were removed from the flooded areas, rather than having time wasted on searching out the few books that might have been unaffected by water. Using sources listed in the plan, restoration paraphernalia were quickly assembled, and included such items as legal pads, marking pens, plastic bags, freezer papers, wrapping tape, milk crates, a roll paper cutter, work tables, pallets, pallet movers, forklifts, and freezer trucks. Portable lights were also brought in to make it possible to work outdoors after dark. Still more book cartons and milk crates were ordered so that books needed to be packed only one layer deep and spine down, to reduce the chance of further damage. For added protection, cartons were stacked only three high, and pallets were not stacked at all. These measures prevented the risk of crushing damaged books. In addition, thirty 300-yard rolls of freezer paper were used; some books were completely wrapped, unnecessarily, on the way to the freezer.

About sixty-five people were employed at any one time; some were library staff and many were volunteers. Supervision was very important, so a leader was appointed for each crew. Workers were carefully instructed on the fragility of both frozen and vacuum-dried books before they were allowed to work.

The narrow stack aisles, which were only 27 inches wide, made it difficult to pack books in cartons. Careful record keeping of the books and their respective order in boxes was not productive in this instance, because books had to be shelved by size in the vacuum chamber to assist drying. Moreover, books had become jammed very tightly into shelves as they expanded when wet. If they had been removed earlier, this would not have been a problem. Freezer trucks were found to be unnecessary, but they might have been important if the run had been hours, instead of minutes long.

All wet materials reached the freezer 43 hours after the start of the emergency, and were safely chilled to −20°F. This halted any deterioration, forestalled the development of mildew, and made possible deliberate consideration of salvage alternatives.

The vacuum chamber selected from those available was the STARS chamber of Lockheed Missiles & Space Co., Inc., at Sunnyvale, located about halfway between the library and the freezer. This is a facility with great capacity ($18 \times 18 \times 36$ ft.), and it is also capable of attaining very low pressures (10^{-3} torr). It has a flat floor, and is well equipped to handle additional instrumentation and the special installations demanded for the vacuum-drying process. Special shelving built to house the books in the vacuum chamber provided a tilt of 12 degrees. Books were shelved upright with spines resting against the warmth of the heating tapes. Experimentation proved that the upright configuration was best, with books placed alongside others of similar size, unwrapped, and supported laterally to prevent covers from warping. Flat shelving was also provided for folio volumes, which dried with less distortion in this position. About 5,000 books were vacuum dried at a time.

When the shelves were loaded and the chamber door was closed, the vacuum was drawn down to well below 4 torr, the critical point above which ice no longer sublimates into water vapor. As the sublimation progressed, water vapor migrated from the books and froze on cryogenic panels. The weight of

Stanford's Meyer Library flood recovery project, 1978–79. Heat and warm water were applied to remove nearly a ton of ice from condenser surfaces after each load of books was processed. *(Photograph courtesy of the Lockheed Missiles & Space Co., Inc.)*

water removed averaged 1,901 pounds per load, or about one-third pound per book.

Weeding out and sorting books at the vacuum chamber was considered and rejected. And fumigation for mildew was impossible to conduct in the chambers. So the decision was made to quarantine the books for four to six weeks for observation. This was done at a vacant school rented for the purpose, where it was also possible to get on with the restoration process and to add moisture to the text block. Books require a content of 5 to 7 percent moisture, and they were leaving the vacuum chamber with 2 percent or less. As it turned out, books that had gone to the freezer did not develop mildew, but some that had been held out as being only slightly dampened, later had to be fumigated to destroy mildew.

Conservation officer Sally Buchanan of Stanford Libraries was responsible for the logistics of the salvage effort: the movement of books from point to point, the procurement of supplies, the recruitment of workers, and the loading and unloading of the vacuum chamber. By unloading the chamber and reloading it the same day, it was possible to finish the whole vacuum process between February 5 and March 12, 1979. There were 51,743 items processed. Because several hundred items in each load required additional drying, nine loads in all were necessary. Separate crews were employed for the two operations at the vacuum chamber. One crew loaded the truck with processed books; another crew met the truck from the freezer, unwrapped frozen books, and placed them on the shelves for vacuum drying. The work of both crews was carried out between 8:30 A.M. and 2:30 P.M. twice a week on working days.

There were some special problems with restoration. "Tinies," miniature books, had been knocked off of shelves into mud during the flooding; they were then frozen into a distorted shape. It was found through experimentation that these books could be partially thawed, then gently manipulated into their proper shape and dried. Leather covers demanded special handling, however, since the wetting, freezing, and drying cycle is unkind to leather. Long-term humidification at 50 to 60 percent relative humidity, followed by careful oiling, was one treatment used.

Another problem involved the recurrence of mildew in some books. This was solved by using thymol crystals and a 30-gallon garbage can with a lock-on lid. Books were suspended open on nylon lines in the can, which also contained a damp towel and the thymol crystals. They stayed there for up to five days. Spending time in this can was also found to benefit leather bindings hardened by water exposure. It softened the leather and conditioned it for cleaning and dressing. If left too long, however, the leather deteriorated.

Coated papers responded well to the vacuum process, except for a small number that proved difficult to unstick. One method used with success involved rewetting, freezing, and then exposing stuck papers to the defrosting cycle of a microwave oven. But this had to be done with skill, since glues melted into the text block rather quickly. When the sticking was due to animal glues washed into the text, the microwave melted the glue, and the quick and dextrous use of hand tools separated the stuck pages.

Old 16mm motion picture film that became wet during the flooding was placed in distilled water for 48 hours, then successfully processed and restored at a photo lab, except for a small portion that had been exposed to the flooding the longest.

Another important insight was received on the first day that the vacuum chamber was used. Considerable interference with the project occurred when news people wandered into the chamber, bent on interviewing the busy workers; they even started pulling fragile books out of the shelves. Their zeal was not anticipated in the planning of the restoration, and a memorandum could have prevented their interference by orienting the media to the project.

Restoration and small repairs to books were carried out over a period of six months at the school site in Palo Alto, then moved into a vacant Stanford laboratory, where the final 5,000 books were repaired. Pamphlet covers were replaced, spines were lettered, and portfolios were made. Only 34 books finally were discarded out of the 52,000 that became wet in the flooding.

Disaster Preparedness

A program of disaster prevention and preparedness for libraries of the University of California is described by Hilda Bohem in a 1978 pamphlet.[6] A product of the university's Task Group on the Preservation of Library Materials, it fills the need for a model plan offering various options, and is usable by any library. A distinctive feature of this plan is that it calls for the establishment of two groups: the Disaster Prevention Team and the Disaster Action Team. The points listed below are suggested by the University of California plan and by other plans, primarily that of the Stanford University Libraries.[7]

    Make a disaster plan for the library, using the plans of others as models; include all pertinent local references.

    Provide disaster action persons with copies of Peter Waters' manual, *Procedures for the Salvage of Water-Damaged Library Materials,* and also place copies in designated emergency boxes within the library.

    Make a complete telephone list, and keep it up to date. Include the phone numbers of library personnel, mechanics, plumbers, electricians, and other key persons whose services may be important in an emergency. Also list available local and regional resources in preservation, as well as the Preservation Office at the Library of Congress, for counsel at the time of disaster and before. When a revised list is issued, discard the old one, since there is a high risk of the new one being discarded in favor of the old list.

    Set priorities for the library in case it becomes necessary to choose immediately between saving one area or one collection ahead of another. Place the shelflist high on the priority list; better still, store a duplicate list in another place. Maintain charts of all areas, illustrating priorities. Also draw up a list of priorities for abandonment. What items would not justify the cost of salvage and could be written off without great harm to the library?

    Identify and list sources of emergency supplies and tools, and work out arrangements or contracts to enlist these sources in the library's plan.

6. Hilda Bohem, *Disaster Prevention and Disaster Preparedness* (Berkeley: Univ. of California Press, 1978).

7. Sally Buchanan, "Disaster Planning," in *Disasters, Prevention and Coping* (Stanford, Calif.: Stanford Univ. Libraries, 1981), pp. 164–67.

Chart 2. Book Restoration Project Flow Chart

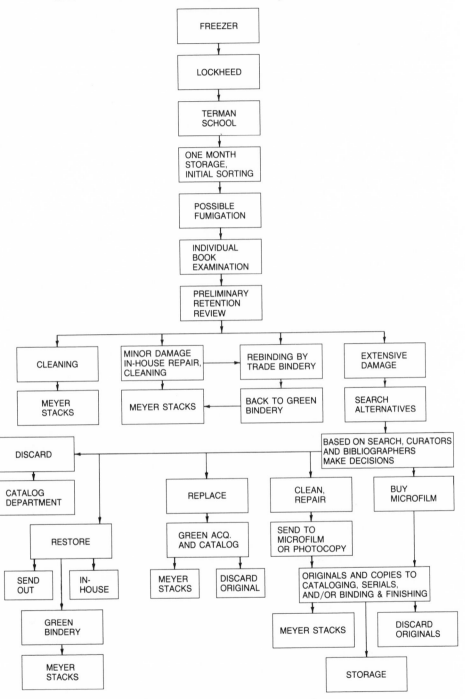

Drawn by conservator Sally Buchanan, showing the many steps possible for books as they were moved through various processing points on their way back to the stacks.

Include or have available such items as generators, pumps, trucks, fork-lifts, pallets and pallet movers, freezer space, cartons or milk crates, freezer wrap, fans, dehumidifiers,[8] fumigators, book carts, an instrument to measure humidity within a book and another to measure tempera-ture and humidity in the building, plastic sheets to protect bookshelves from water, an industrial type wet-or-dry vacuum cleaner and mop-up gear, and some clean newsprint to help with air drying. A stopper for a working automatic sprinkler head should be available for use when a fire is under control.

Make sure staff members know how to turn off electrical, water, and gas lines if it becomes necessary to do so, or who must be called to take care of these duties.

Set up an accounting system for any emergency; this will simplify both the insurance claims and the recovery program.

Following are some recommendations on how to take action in the event of a water disaster:

Be wary of making hasty decisions. If the library's disaster plan has been kept up to date, staff will be able to make the right moves in the right order.

Consider safety of people first. In a water emergency, watch out for elec-trical (electrocution) hazards in a flooded building; also watch out for very slippery footing.

Inform the library's insurance carrier or agent of the incident at the earliest moment possible. Assess the damage carefully and logically, with the direct assistance of persons who know the materials and the values involved. Take pictures.

After the first assessment of the damage, retreat to a quiet place to decide on a plan of action. Explain the situation to experts by telephone or in person, and ask their advice.

After fire or flood, vent the building as promptly as possible. Break win-dows, if necessary, to vent smoke and to reduce humidity. Circulate the air with fans; if the power is out, bring in portable generators to power fans. It is not true that the humidity level will drop if the tem-perature is raised; this only enhances the growth of mold.

If the disaster has removed part of the library's roof, cover the books promptly with salvage covers or plastic sheets to limit damage.

If large amounts of materials are wet, try to move them into a freezer, wrapped sufficiently to prevent them from sticking to each other. Place the books spine down, one layer deep, and freeze them to −20°F or colder.

Air dry books that are only slightly damp; place them head down, fanned slightly open, on clean newsprint in a cool, dry place. Interleave pages

---

8. A Houston, Texas, entrepreneur, Don Hartsell (doing business as Airdex), uses an oversized dehumidifier to pump super-dry air into a building and pull out quantities of water. It was used with success at the Walter Branch of the Houston Public Library, after a rainstorm flooded the library during roof repair.

with clean newsprint or paper towelling, changing papers as they become damp. Keep air moving and ambient humidity as low as possible.

Fumigation or another fungicidal procedure may become necessary if mildew develops in large areas.[9]

For water damage to films, slides, or photographs, alert the photo lab to the problem, then immerse items in distilled water until they can be taken to the lab for restoration.

Flat materials can be dried between sheets of newsprint or between blotters; handle art materials with extreme care.

Leave submerged books or books floating in water in the water until they can be packed off to a freezer; this reduces the opportunity for mildew to develop.

Avoid making hasty decisions about discarding materials, if possible; they may be salvageable.

All floors contaminated by smoke and water must be scrubbed with a formalin solution or another mold inhibitor; use recommended precautions when using these and other toxic materials.

9. Ethylene oxide, used sometimes as a fungicide, is flammable and has an explosive range of 3 to 80 percent in air. It must be used with the greatest care to avoid explosion and fire. Use in any confined space invites an explosion. It is not only toxic and a severe irritant to the respiratory tract and lungs but also a source of severe dermatitis.

6 Planning and Design for Safety and Security

In a well-wrought interior design every single detail is laden with thought.[1]

Henry Dreyfuss, well known as a designer of airplane interiors and other things, argued that design is good or bad according to the way it accommodates or inconveniences people. "When the point of contact between the product and the user becomes a point of friction," he said, "then the designer has failed."[2] In the library setting, there are many details that can directly affect the convenience and safety of people and the preservation of the collections.

A newsletter editor, describing his visit to the modern art gallery and library of a leading university, warned his readers, "Watch out for its main staircase, which goes up treacherously on a bias and down which I fell flat, half an hour before I was to speak on lunacy and the arrangement of books. . . ."[3] Ellsworth Mason finds circular stairs ornamental; but besides taking up more space than other configurations, they "inflict a constant, if slight, discomfort on users" and require a schizophrenic choice between giant strides and mincing steps.[4] For a fuller discussion of this problem, refer to the National Fire Protection Association rules for stair design, which are given in the following section.

Some of the information on planning and design can be seen in other chapters. But the purpose of this chapter is to bring attention to design details that tend to be inadequately worked out in library buildings. Some are listed because of negative comments that have come from librarians and design critics. Others relate to actual injuries, accidents, or unpleasant incidents. Three examples follow:

> A library staff person descending a stairway fell and suffered severe injuries; there was no handrail on the wall side, only on the open side of the staircase.

1. Ellsworth Mason, "A Well-Wrought Interior Design," *Library Journal* 92 (Feb. 1967):743
2. Henry Dreyfuss, *Designing for People* (New York: Simon and Schuster, 1955), 23.
3. *BiN Bibliographic Newsletter* 11 (March/April 1983):1–2.
4. Ellsworth Mason, *Mason on Library Buildings* (Metuchen, N.J.: Scarecrow Press, 1980), 245.

University City (Missouri) Public Library. Here the architect achieves a curve in the stairway without curving the treads.

A guard railing on a stair landing had uprights (balusters) spaced only slightly further apart than the recommended standard six-inch spacing. A child fell through the railing and landed on an employee, who was injured. The child was unhurt.

Numerous injuries and a few fatalities have occurred from the unwise use of plate glass in large partition and wall panels. Architects have frequently overlooked the potential for disaster in this handsome but deceptive construction.

Planning for Safety

Most of the suggestions that follow are supported by codes and standards or accidents or losses directly related to details of design.

Glass

Plate glass used unwisely has accounted for many accidents and injuries in public buildings. People tend to walk or run into large panels of glass which, for one optical reason or another, are not perceived for what they are. Injuries tend to be severe. As a result, model building codes, such as the Uniform Building Code and the code of the Building Officers' Conference of America, have ruled out the use of glass larger than six feet square in fixed glass panels that are subject to human impact, unless the glass is plate glass fully protected by a push bar or protective screen, or divided by a muntin, or unless the glass is laminated, fully tempered, or wired.

Any large structural glass panels extending to the floor or close to it are liable to be a source of injuries. Typically they soon have to be barricaded with potted plants or furniture, or posted with decals or etched with patterns to make them more visible. Another construction inviting injury is the placing of fixed glass panels adjacent to glass doors of very similar size and shape, a deception to be avoided.

Stairs

A National Fire Protection Association rule describes an approved curved stair design as one that has a 10-inch minimum depth of tread and a minimum radius of not less than twice the measurement of the depth.[5] Thus, a tread might be 11 inches in depth at the narrower end and not less than 22 inches in the long dimension. This design is accepted in the *Life Safety Code* as a component in a means of egress, i.e., as part of a route for travel to an exit in time of emergency.

Equally important, any openwork or uprights in guard rails on stairs, landings, or mezzanines should prevent a 6-inch sphere from passing through.[6] This design will prevent a child from squeezing through between uprights and falling. Tests have indicated that $5^{1}/_{2}$ inches is an even better standard.

For stair handrails, consider the beauty and convenience of smooth, round, metal tubing $1^{1}/_{2}$ to $2^{1}/_{2}$ inches in diameter; it can be articulated into the continuous handrail required by American National Standards Institute standards for the convenience of the blind, and is popular with others as well. Massive stone or timber handrails, while esthetically striking, do not provide as good a grip for the hands, particularly arthritic hands and those of children.

Stair handrails are sometimes carried across a level landing to serve as a guard railing at the same height (usually 34 inches) as the handrail on the stairs; this height is inadequate. The guard rail instead should be 42 inches high.

Handrails are needed on both sides of any stairs, not on just the open side. They should extend the entire length of the stair and should never terminate before reaching a landing or a floor level. Monumental stairs need one or more intermediate handrails.

Avoid having a single step difference in levels inside or outside the building; it causes falls and injuries.

Finally, an enclosed fire stairway built around an open well in a multistory library seems to tempt users into dropping books from a height. A simple return stair design, if it can be accommodated, requires less space and reduces the possibility of such incidents.

Lights

If possible, avoid using recessed lights, also called "down lights," that project a bright circle of light on the floor and leave the rest of the area in semi-darkness.

---

5. National Fire Protection Association, *NFPA 101, Life Safety Code* (Quincy, Mass.: NFPA, 1985), p. 14.

6. *NFPA 101, Life Safety Code,* p. 16.

The ideal handrail, metal tubing articulated between levels; main library, University of California at Santa Cruz. *(Photograph courtesy of Tom Walters.)*

When planning to install manual or automatic alarm systems, consider the possibility of using visible (flashing light) signals for persons who may be present in such places as listening rooms or music rooms, where the soundproofing and background noise would prevent them from hearing an audible alarm or an emergency public address announcement.

A library handrail of clean design, but presenting the user with uncomfortable sharp angles and points.

Intermediate handrails are recommended on all wide stairways and are required by various building codes.

A single step between levels is awkward; here it has been marked with hazard striping, then modified with a wheelchair ramp.

Entrances and Exits
Be careful to consider the needs of the handicapped, especially when planning entryways. Wheelchair access to the building and to rest rooms is now required by law. In addition, you will need to use both braille markings and raised Arabic numerals in elevators and at elevator landings since braille is not familiar to the majority of the blind population.

If a main exit has several doors located side by side, provide a large push plate, handle, or "panic bar" not more than half the width of the door so that people have no difficulty seeing where to push.

Planning for Security

Building security can be promoted by the physical design and layout of the building itself, through detection devices that ward off or warn of intruders, and through inexpensive commonsense measures. Some of these safeguards are discussed below.

Interior Design
The interior layout of the library should provide maximum visibility of public areas to facilitate surveillance, particularly where rare books and other valuable materials may be handled by patrons. To promote visibility, avoid arranging the stacks in rows that create concealed aisles, if possible. Also avoid using part-height walls and partitions; extending them to the ceiling improves security for offices and other rooms.

Locate rest rooms in convenient and well-traveled areas to facilitate supervision and to discourage illicit activities.

Whether the stacks are open or closed, it should be possible to design the library so that there is one controlled exit through which all library users must pass.[7]

Air handling systems, skylights, and other construction features requiring openings in a roof or walls should be made vandal-resistant. The intake duct for an air handling system should be so located that vandals cannot easily reach it to introduce fire, smoke, or other hazards into the building.

It is also important to have emergency lighting for stairways and central areas during a power failure. Local or self-contained emergency lighting units have certain advantages over a system dependent on a central generator designed to go into action when the normal power fails: (1) each unit can be tested at any time by pressing a button; (2) each unit is a complete system, continually recharging itself from the normal building circuit, and dependent for action only on the failure of that power supply; (3) there is no danger of failure to perform resulting from the destruction of a circuit, such as has occurred more than once with large buildings that are protected by a central gen-

7. Stephen Langmead and Margaret Beckman, *New Library Design; Guide-Lines to Planning Academic Library Buildings* (New York, John Wiley & Sons, 1970), p. 28.

erator system; and (4) semi-portable battery units are relatively inexpensive and easy to repair and replace.

Elevators

Plan a system for controlling elevators against unauthorized use, particularly after hours. Consult with the elevator installer or maintenance contractor to work out emergency routines to follow during a power failure. Post instructions and emergency procedures in the elevator(s).

Doors and Windows

Windows provide opportunity for intrusion and vandalism; if you are planning a new building or major alterations, consider using windowless construction on one or more sides of the building. In addition to providing security, this design offers books protection from (ultraviolet) sunlight. The new building of the Newberry Library has this design.

Install security screens on openable windows to prevent book thieves from dropping books outside. Crank-out casement windows will require screens inside rather than outside. Consider using vandal-resistant security glazing for rear

Chicago's Newberry Library incorporates the benefits of superior climate control and security in a windowless addition built in 1982. *(Photograph courtesy of Newberry Library.)*

windows and for those that are concealed from the street, if not for all windows that are accessible from the ground. Whether the product is intended for vandal-resistance or for protection against windstorm, fire, or intrusion, keep in mind that the strength of the barrier varies considerably with the product selected. The following questions should be asked of the architect or the supplier:

> Is the space to be glazed too large for the thickness of the glazing and the edge engagement?
>
> Is polycarbonate glazing the best for the library's needs, or would a glass-clad polycarbonate be better?
>
> Is laminated safety glass advised?
>
> Will the product resist burning with a torch, or the application of chemicals or solvents?
>
> Will it burn?
>
> What kind of impact is needed to break through it?

If a rear door is needed, consider installing one that will discourage casual vandals; a steel-clad door without exposed hinges is best to use for this purpose. If glass is used in an exterior door, install a double cylinder deadbolt lock that requires a key to open the door from either side. A deadbolt is especially effective if an oversized strike plate is installed to accommodate the bolt. If panic bolts are required on certain exit doors, special attention may be needed to prevent unauthorized entry after hours, and unauthorized exit for stealing books or other materials. Public safety officials may be of help in this area. The time-delay panic bolt is one possible solution; another is the installation of an electromagnetic door system.

Where several exit doors are side by side in a principal exitway, the design sometimes does not indicate where to push to open a door. There should be an obvious indication in the form of a large push plate, handle, or "panic bar" extending across only part of the door, to the extent that this is acceptable to local authorities.

Security Devices

Consider using convex industrial safety mirrors to facilitate the surveillance of remote areas.[8] Also consider the installation of closed circuit television for the surveillance of remote areas and special collections. This is one way of watching emergency exit doors when someone is making use of them for theft or in violation of a posted notice limiting the door to emergency use only. With suitable equipment, a videotape can be made of activity in almost any area of the library.

Another valuable device is an electronic intrusion alarm system with central station monitoring, which defends against burglary, vandalism, and incendiary fires. Also available are window screens designed to send a signal over the intrusion alarm circuit when tampered with.

8. Frank J. DeRosa, "The Disruptive Patron," *Library & Archival Security* 3 (Winter 1980):29–37.

Outdoor Security

Avoid building an outdoor reading terrace; the books tend to "walk away" with the readers.[9] Plan shrubbery with pedestrian safety in mind, so as to deprive muggers of a means of concealment. If experience warrants it, consider installing an emergency telephone in the parking lot, a one-purpose circuit to handle calls for help. Finally, illuminate outdoor areas by providing vandal-resistant flood-lights for parking lots and access walks into the library.[10]

Site

An isolated site increases the likelihood of vandalism and burning; therefore, a library so located has an increased need for automatic detection and suppression systems. Two studies made in England and a number of fires in the United States attest to this.[11] When a building is quite close to another, the potential for fire in the library resulting from fire in the other building should be weighed carefully. A blank masonry wall facing the other building would be one good defense.[12]

Fire

Building Design   A hallmark of the modern multistory library is the opening of two or more floors with a well or an atrium, gaining a pleasing sense of interior spaciousness at the cost of a considerable expense in floor space. Since the open plan does away with the horizontal fire divisions provided by floors, the fire protection problem is not as simple as it would otherwise be. To cite one example, Bobst Library of New York University, one of the earliest libraries of atrium design, has a "shower wall" plan of protection. Ten floor levels are separated from the open interior by a partition of wired glass backed by a line of automatic sprinklers. The fire risk in the atrium is also controlled by excluding such furniture as overstuffed chairs and sofas.

Wells and atriums are esthetically appealing, but they reduce the available floor space and deprive the building of the flexibility of modular design to some extent. Even if the fire risk is well controlled, the atrium may open various levels to unwanted and disturbing noise levels, much more so than in the conventional compartmented building. These aspects need to be anticipated in the planning.

Compartmentation is a fire protection term referring to the subdividing of a building with fire-resistive and smoke-tight division walls, floors, and stair enclosures. It makes possible the confining of a fire to a small area of the building, and it also makes for good noise control as a side benefit. A fire barrier caulking compound should be used to caulk pipe openings and other penetrations in fire walls and floors; this can also be a do-it-yourself improvement in existing buildings.

If compact shelving and storage systems are in the library's plans, be aware that they greatly increase fuel loading in a building, making automatic sprinkler

9. Keyes D. Metcalf, *Planning Academic and Research Library Buildings* (New York: McGraw-Hill, 1965), p. 78.

10. Marvine Brand, "Security of Academic Buildings," *Library & Archival Security* 3 (Spring 1980):39–47.

11. *Fire Prevention* 144 (Oct., 1981):17.

12. G. P. McKinnon, ed., *Fire Protection Handbook,* 14th ed. (Boston: National Fire Protection Association, 1976)6:114–16.

Broward County's Fort Lauderdale (Florida) Main Library; the lofty atrium is an exciting architectural form, although some quiet for reading and study may be sacrificed. *(Photograph courtesy of Broward County Library System.)*

protection essential if the fire risk is to be kept under control, especially in basement levels, where these systems tend to be placed.

Interior Materials   Intumescent paints remarkably increase the resistance of a wood structure to fire. Properly applied and maintained, they react in fire with a blistering action, forming a barrier that temporarily but effectively delays

In 1983 installation was completed of 55 miles of mobile compact storage in the sixth stack addition to the General Library, University of Illinois, Champaign-Urbana. *(Rendering Courtesy of Lankton, Ziegele, Terry and Associates, Inc.)*

the spread of fire. Other materials are also available for use as fire retardants.

Be careful in choosing an interior finish and furnishings. Some of these materials burn very fast and create dense smoke, and certain plastics even aggravate fire damage. Imitation wood veneer paneling is liable to be dangerously fast burning; examine and test it by burning before deciding to install it.

Where plastic foam insulation is used, it can be made fire safe by sealing it with a cement-type, Underwriters' Laboratories listed product applied with a spray gun applicator. Similarly, ordinary plate glass can be reinforced with a transparent plastic film that will give it impact resistance, prevent flying splinters if the glass is broken, and vastly increase its resistance to heat and fire. Look for a listing by a known testing laboratory, and recognize the limitations of the protection being provided.

Water

Conducting regular maintenance and inspection routines is probably the most important way of protecting buildings against water damage. The points that follow are some that can be considered in the planning and design stage for new construction or alterations.

General Considerations In earthquake country, it is important to provide sturdy construction in order to prevent water casualties and other forms of damage. This will include sway bracing of water system piping and the securing of book shelves at the top and bottom, as discussed in an earlier chapter.

In hurricane and tornado regions, libraries should have the benefit of construction details that have proved successful in reducing wind and water damage to buildings and their contents, particularly to roofs and windows. Consider installing special impact-resistant glazing on windows to reduce the risk of breakage by windborne debris.

Avoid outside stair and window well constructions leading into levels below ground level, which may collect water and divert it into the building.

Pipes and Drains Water damage also may result from poorly constructed or poorly located pipes and drains. Make sure that the floor drains are actually in the lowest points of the floor. In addition, provide a backup pump for basement sump pumps, and list sources of emergency pumps.

Pipe layouts should be designed to prevent electrolysis between adjacent pipes, both inside and outside the building (underground). Insulation for cold water pipes may be needed to prevent drip from condensation in warm and humid weather. Some libraries run gutters under cold water pipes and have water alarms as well.

Roofs In any roof construction the quality of the materials, the design, and the workmanship are of great importance. Libraries should plan for a professional to conduct a final inspection for leaks and imperfections before accepting a job or a new building. Look for drains leading from a flat roof, and make sure

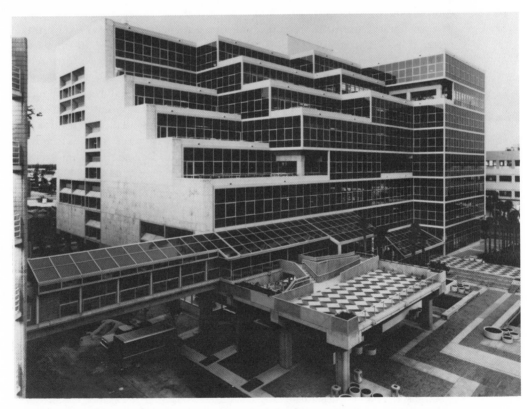

Fort Lauderdale (Florida) Main Library has impact-resistant glazing on lower floors to reduce damage from flying debris in tropical windstorms. *(Photograph courtesy of Stephen Leek.)*

that water from the drains cannot find its way into the building at any point. Also use copper flashing in building a roof, nothing inferior.[13]

Provide for access through the roof for any heavy equipment that may be acquired or removed in the future; one such possibility is a hatchway that can be used with a crane or a helicopter. By all means, avoid the need for moving heavy items across the roof, which may open up cracks.[14]

Warning Devices   Water alarms are available commercially, or they can be fabricated by a library's own mechanics. It is good to invest in such an alarm, but it should be monitored at all hours so as to alert the library at once to any unwanted water in the building. Also make sure that the waterflow alarm in the automatic sprinkler system is functional when the system is placed in operation.

Consultant Services

In any major building or rebuilding project, it is wise to consider using consultant services to obtain the best results. The library building consultant, the security specialist, and the fire protection engineer all have the capacity to avoid errors, effect economies, and take advantage of the poor experience others have had on similar projects. It is recommended that the client organization obtain its own library consultant regardless of the presence of the library consultant retained by the architect. The relationship is not unlike that of attorneys who present two sides in litigation, except that the client's consultant probably will have the last word in any failure to find agreement.[15]

The architect may also want to obtain the advice of a pest control specialist to prevent a projected building from becoming a bird sanctuary. Constructions that make good roosting or nesting places should be avoided. Pigeons not only disfigure a building with droppings but they also carry mites and other vermin, which find their way into the building through window openings and intakes for ventilating ducts.

Environmental concerns, such as lighting and ventilation, that affect both people and collections are especially tough problem areas. The planning team must find the best advice by reading about the shortcomings of earlier buildings and by visiting the better-constructed, newer libraries to obtain empirical evidence, particularly on lighting. Consultant engineering services on heating, ventilation, and air conditioning systems are worth the expense, since so many systems turn out to be inadequate to the complex demands of a library environment.

Always bear in mind that objectivity is of the utmost importance. It can be achieved only if the consultant is not obligated in any way to any supplier, manufacturer, or installer. Be frank in asking if the consultant has any such ties.

13. Ellen Watts, "The Mayer Center of the Phillips Exeter Academy," *Technology and Conservation* 3 (Fall 1982):20–31.

14. Philip D. Leighton, "Reducing Preservation Hazards within Library Facilities," *Disasters, Prevention and Coping* (Stanford, Calif.: Stanford University Libraries 1980), pp. 32–40.

15. Ellsworth Mason, *Mason on Libraries*, pp. 4, 8.

7 Preservation and Conservation

Like Noah, we have a big mess in the bottom of the ark, and unless it's brought under control soon, the collections that are the lifeblood of our civilization will be lost to the future as surely as was the world before the Flood.[1]

Paper chemistry, the decay of 19th- and 20th-century papers, and the continuing programs of deacidification, microforming, and certain other facets of preservation, while important, are beyond the depth and scope of this book. What follows in this chapter is a brief and necessarily oversimplified account of some of the problems libraries have in controlling the deleterious influences and agents that affect library materials

Problems

Temperature and Humidity
Books are similar to food products in their need for a cold, dark storage environment to prevent or retard deterioration. Because of this, strict environmental controls in book storage may one day be as commonly accepted as refrigeration for food. A temperature of 60°F (15.6°C), plus or minus 5 degrees or even colder, is recommended for book storage spaces.[2] Yet the juxtaposition of open stacks and reading rooms in libraries makes it difficult to maintain an ideal stacks temperature. Humidity recommended is 50 percent, with a tolerance of 3 percent up or down in diurnal variation, and 6 percent up or down in seasonal variation.

New libraries may find that their planning was inadequate for temperature and humidity controls. Double window or storm window construction needs to be tight, and a moisture barrier must be engineered into the design to maintain relative humidity at 50 percent, or lower, at 45 percent, plus or minus 5 percent, as some experts prefer. For proper temperature control, the design should in-

1. Pamela W. Darling, "Will Anything Be Left? New Responses to the Preservation Challenge," *Wilson Library Bulletin* 56 (Nov. 1981):178.
2. Paul N. Banks, "Environmental Standards for Storage of Books and Manuscripts," *Library Journal* (Feb. 1974):340.

The 1982 addition of the Newberry Library was designed with environmental controls as a primary requirement. Air pollution, humidity, temperature, and light are strictly monitored and regulated. *(Photograph courtesy of Newberry Library.)*

corporate a plan for superior insulation against summer heat and winter cold; any extra expense that results from this plan will shortly be recovered in savings from lowered heating and cooling costs.

Air Quality

Both dust and gaseous pollutants should be removed from air circulated through the library. Particulates can be removed in a well-engineered air handling system at a filtering efficiency of 90 percent. But sulfur dioxide, ozone, and oxides of nitrogen also need to be extracted from library air. This a more complex problem than removing the dust. Although at present there is no universally approved method, it is expected that one will be discovered with continuing research into preferred methods.[3]

Lighting

All light degrades paper. Ultraviolet light is the most damaging, whether it comes from sunshine, daylight, or fluorescent lighting. Daylight can be filtered to remove ultraviolet light by using rigid sheets or flexible film designed to cover windows. Likewise, interior lighting can be subdued through the use of filtering sleeves placed over the tubes; the sleeve can outlast several tubes, but eventually loses its effectiveness and has to be replaced. Other ways of reducing exposure to light include replacing fluorescent lights with incandescent lamps, keeping

3. Paul N. Banks, correspondence, Sept. 1985.

lighting always at the lowest level compatible with need, and turning off lights when they are not actually needed. Such control of lighting also produces real savings. For example, the University of South Carolina, which has a floor area in the library of about $7^1/_2$ acres, installed a lighting control system that saves the university $90,660 annually by switching off 28,000 lights at times when they are not actually needed.[4]

Exhibit cases present special problems in lighting and ventilation. The materials displayed are frequently very valuable, rare, and fragile. Any light source within the case might cause damage through heating. Low level incandescent light can be received from outside the case, but not from a spotlight, since it tends to produce heat through infrared radiation. Some movement of filtered air is needed throughout the case, and a 30-day limit is recommended for the display of any highly valued item.

Pests

Yale's libraries have had some instructive experience with pests, commencing with an infestation of beetles in rare, imported late 16th-century European books.[5] The libraries set beetle traps made of glass crystallizing dishes 70mm across and 50mm high, containing wheat flour as bait and coated with white flour paste on the outside to give the insects good footing. Five species were trapped in this way, the most numerous of which were *Anobiidae*, known variously as the deathwatch beetle, the powder post beetle, and the shot hole borer. Other trapped insects included the *Bostrichidae* (a flying beetle), a single *Dermestid*, book lice, and book mites. Altogether, 37,000 books were in the infested area.

Looking for an ideal method of extermination, library staff took the advice of a professor of biology, who suggested freezing the books. The results were good. They then built for $10,000 a 368 cubic foot blast freezer in the lower stacks of Beinicke Library and processed the books in it, about 400 at a time, chilling them for three days at $-20°F$ ($-29°C$). Books were placed in plastic bags to prevent condensation during the defrosting process. The library now routinely deep-freezes any new acquisitions that are suspected of harboring pests. Another excellent use made of the freezer is the freezing of wet books after a water incident, a standard restoration procedure.

European insects are not the only pests that get into books. Cockroaches, silverfish, and firebrats are all attracted by food, and will eat one or more ingredients of books as well. These indigenous pests are said to be vulnerable to a sprinkling of boric acid powder on dry surfaces where they are active, or to a powder blend of pyrethrum flowers and sodium fluoride, or to spraying with parathion, malathion, or pyrethrum.[6] Book lice (psocids), once considered harmless to books, are now known to damage paper. Their presence indicates a damp area or environment. If the humidity is reduced to 50 percent and any damp refuge is removed, the book lice will disappear.

4. *Library Journal* 109 (April 1984):619.

5. Gay Walker, "The Quiet Disaster II: Pests and People," in *Disasters, Prevention and Coping* (Stanford, Calif.: Stanford University Libraries, 1981), pp. 24 ff.

6. George Martin Cunha, "The Care of Books and Documents," in Codicologica 5, *Les matériaux du livre manuscrit* (Leiden: E. J. Brill, 1980), p. 70.

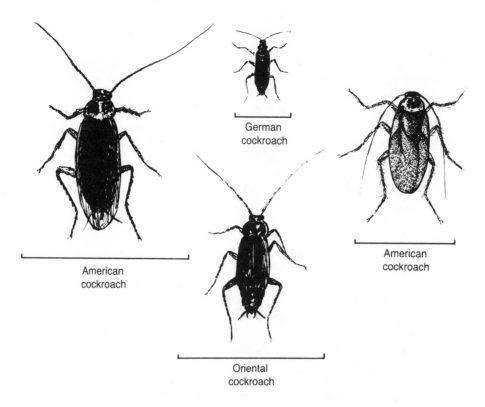

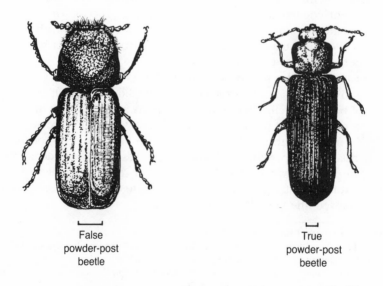

Destructive insects sometimes found in books. The bar below each sketch indicates the actual size of the adult insect. Sketches by Carol Williams.

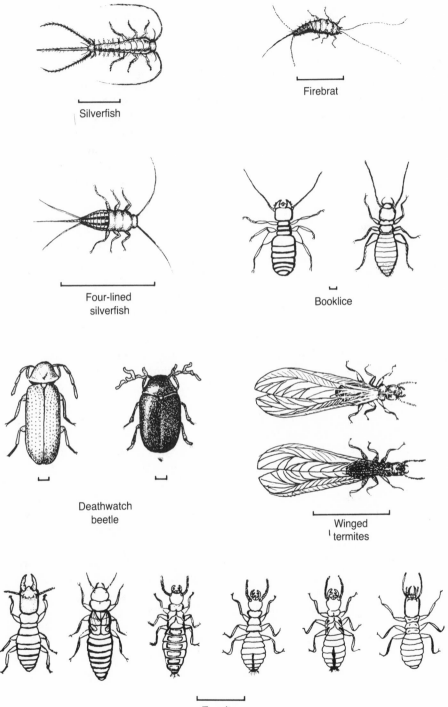

Silverfish

Firebrat

Four-lined
silverfish

Booklice

Deathwatch
beetle

Winged
termites

Termites

Rats and mice also can be very damaging. Rat-proofing floor, wall, and pipe openings is recommended, as are the services of a reliable exterminator. An aggressive cat can be employed for mouse control.

People

Academic libraries, probably more than others, suffer from the outrageous abuse of library books. Yale was plagued for a time by a "roof book phantom" who selected choice 17th-century books from the stacks and threw them out of upper windows to crash on roofs below, usually during a rain or snow storm. This method has also been widely used by book thieves; it suggests the need for some arrangement that would prevent the passing of books out of windows. Almost any university library staff could match the Yale experience with anecdotes of their own.

Another kind of abuse is usually not deliberate, but damaging nonetheless. This is the negligent handling and processing of books by staff persons in the library. Gentleness in the handling, shelving, and storing of books is most important. Bookends are needed to support backs and prevent warping. Books also need to be carefully manipulated on and off shelves and over bookends to avoid abrasion. Book carts, conveyors, and mechanical equipment all have a potential for damaging books, and should therefore be lined, padded, and maintained with this problem in mind.

Other hazards include mending books with pressure-sensitive tapes, unprofessional mending of any kind, and lack of care when packing books for interlibrary shipment. Rare books are sometimes damaged when they are set up for exhibit without proper support, which strains the hinges and lets the textblock fall forward.

Because of the popularity of photocopying machines, books are routinely being subjected to a kind of back-breaking stress. To insure a sharp copy, the user will spread a book open, then lean on it heavily to make sure the textblock is pressed flat against the glass top of the machine. This is harsh treatment for the spine and binding; and the older the book, the greater the damage to it from cracking and overstressing the binding. Furthermore, the page or pages being copied are subjected briefly to a brilliant light; this, too, is a less than beneficial treatment, particularly for older books, and the more so for pages that can be expected to be copied many times in a few years.

Certainly, libraries need to be educating users on these points. Makers of the photocopying machines are already recognizing the problem by improving their equipment. At least one model sold in England is designed to protect books, and it is likely that one or more improved machines are available from U.S. distributors.[7] Libraries can also protect their choice books by making copies for users and/or by making master copies of pages that are in demand so that subsequent copies do not require the use of the book itself.

7. Bernard Williams, "The Selected Duo Copy: a Book Copier Developed for the British Library," *Information Media and Technology* 18 (Winter 1985):26–27.

Remedies

Housekeeping in Bookstacks

The regular cleaning of bookstacks prevents the deterioration of books. Vellum covers can be lightly wiped with the waterless suds from saddle soap. Leather-bound volumes should be cleaned at 18- to 24-month intervals, again using the frothy suds of saddle soap (not wet), and immediately wiped off; this cleaning should be followed by an appropriate treatment to inhibit mold and mildew, if they are problems. Leather bindings require a good deal of care as each binding is different. Conservators are now cautious about recommending oiling; some bindings need a penetrating oil, some a hard surface treatment, and so on.[8]

Termites are not often mentioned as enemies of books, but there have been destructive infestations of them in libraries. If termites are known to be in the building, any wood bookshelves should be moved away from walls and stood on metal plates or set into dishes of coal tar or creosote. Termites are well organized; therefore, the services of a professional exterminator are recommended.

In a building where climate control is inadequate and mold and mildew may be present, a fungicide may be needed. Thymol has been used as a fungicide, but there may be better materials available. The University of Illinois had success with a product (Dowicide) suggested by the Preservation Office in the Library of Congress. In crystalline powder form, "this chemical vaporizes at room temperature, is much less expensive and less toxic than thymol, and can be quite simply deposited over a large affected area." The advice of the manufacturer of such a product should be solicited and closely followed.[9]

A National Program

The desirability of establishing a national preservation program has been discussed for some time, and there has been some progress. Reports were produced in 1964 by Gordon Williams and in 1972 by Warren J. Haas for the association of Research Libraries, proposing cooperative action at the national level. In 1976, plans of the Library of Congress were announced, calling for the following actions:

I. Microfilming of valued materials that are too brittle for ordinary handling, and retention of the contents on master negatives stored under ideal conditions.

II. Preservation of the contents of rare and valuable materials in the nation's libraries by expert paper conservators, the establishment of a comprehensive training program to prepare conservators, and finally, the establishment of regional conservation centers similar to the Northeast Document Conservation Center at Andover, Massachusetts.

III. Preservation, in one way or another, of present and future publications of value now being printed on paper that has a life expectancy of fifty years or less.[10]

8. Paul N. Banks, correspondence, Sept. 1985.

9. Univ. of Illinois Library Friends at Champaign–Urbana, "Staff Rescues Books from Mold," *Friend-script* 3 (Summer 1981):2.

10. Frazer G. Poole, "The Proposed National Preservation Program of the Library of Congress," *Library Journal* 101 (Nov. 1976):2351.

Part I of the national program is being implemented by a subgroup from the Research Libraries Group. Under a substantial grant from the Andrew W. Mellon Foundation and the National Endowment for the Humanities, an ambitious cooperative microfilming preservation project is being carried out. The group consists of the libraries of six universities: Columbia, Yale, Brown, Michigan, Minnesota, and California (Berkeley), plus the New York Public Library. The Library of Congress is also a participant. The undertaking concerns a target group of materials in U.S. imprints and Americana from the worst years of the "bad paper" period, 1875–1900.

Library of Congress Resources

A key element in the program and a ready source of assistance available to any library is the National Preservation Program Office in the Library of Congress in Washington, D.C. This is a relatively new office with a very broad assignment of responsibility—to respond to the needs of libraries everywhere. The staff is dedicated to service and will respond to requests for information received by telephone or letter.

There is even room for a "Jane Doe" service in that the person calling need not be a librarian, but can be any private person needing advice or information in the area of preservation or conservation. The office generally does not send out consultant personnel for emergency aid where fire and water have struck, as was done a few times in the past, but they can advise a library about preservationists and facilities for recovery available in any region of the country.

Other services of the National Preservation Program Office include internships, workshops, seminars, tours, and participation in the cooperative microfilming project. Audiovisual instruction materials are also loaned out. In addition, a series of leaflets on topics in preservation and conservation has been popular and is being continued.

Part II of the national program is making progress slowly, so training courses for library conservators still are few. The two-year program at Columbia University's School of Library Service, followed by a one-year internship at a recognized conservation laboratory, is the first full-fledged program. There are also some graduate training opportunities in museum conservation that may contribute to library needs; these are offered by the New York University Institute of Fine Arts, the University of Delaware, and the State University of New York College at Buffalo.

A Model Regional Program

The national program calls for the eventual establishment of regional conservation centers. Although this has not come about, it seems possible that the universities themselves will eventually fill this role. The model for such centers has been the Northeast Document Conservation Center (formerly the New England Document Conservation Center). Originally provided space by the Merrimack Valley Textile Museum at North Andover, Massachusetts, it soon outgrew the building and moved to Abbot Hall in Andover.

The center came into being in 1973 as a shared facility that cares for the needs of client institutions that lack their own conservation facilities. It also serves as a model for the establishment of other centers. It was incorporated in 1980 as a nonprofit organization serving New England, New York, and New Jersey.

There is a full-time staff of thirty, fifteen of whom are conservators. Internships in conservation are available for students who have completed degree work in this field, with an emphasis on paper conservation.

The clientele are the 300 institutions, more or less, who call upon the center every year for counsel and services. Both routine and emergency field services are offered. Representatives also conduct seminars and workshops for libraries; and the field service director surveys libraries to make recommendations for fire protection, water protection, climate control, binding methods, storage, lighting, and electrical services. Another very important service is disaster assistance. Any library that is struck by a water or fire disaster can receive telephoned instructions and on-site counsel from field workers from the center.

The center now specializes in the conservation of library and archival materials, and works of art on paper. During its first ten years, services were performed for more than 800 museums, libraries, and historical societies. The paper conservation laboratory handles not only books and documents, but also maps and architectural drawings. High quality microfilming is done, as is the transfer of images from decaying and flammable nitrate film to a safer, more permanent medium. In both paper and photo conservation, the center offers not only treat-

A modern miracle: a machine imported from Israel fills holes in paper to restore a worm-eaten page. Field Service Director Mildred O'Connell of the Northeast Document Conservation Center shows a restored page alongside a damaged page. *(Photograph courtesy of Northeast Document Conservation Center.)*

ment and processing of materials, but also consultations, workshops, and seminars.

Rare and fragile ancient books are given the most painstaking care. Some are disbound, and the pages are immersed in water and carefully washed, deacidified, resewn, and rebound by hand. Promoting permanence and durability takes precedence over producing an exact facsimile or a decorative binding. If insects have drilled holes in the pages, the pages can be restored by the Recurator, a remarkable machine manufactured in Israel and one of only six in existence.[11]

Following are some examples of the center's outstanding performance to date. More than seventy years after the great fire that destroyed the New York State Library in 1911, books damaged in the fire were sent to the Northeast Document Conservation Center, where they were successfully repaired. Another project was the restoration of the map General Pershing used in his field headquarters during World War I, restored at the request of the U.S. Military Academy at West Point. The center has also restored a draft of a poem pencilled by Emily Dickinson, survey drawings by Henry Thoreau, the architectural drawings of Frank Lloyd Wright, the log of the *U.S.S. Constitution,* and any number of historic documents and rare books. As new centers for cooperative conservation are planned and organized, they will have an excellent model in the leadership provided by the Northeast Document Conservation Center.

Evidence of progress in Part III of the National Preservation Program is a massive deacidificaton project. This is a 30-year program in which the Library of Congress will treat one million books each year in a DEZ (diethyl zinc) procedure, neutralizing excess acid, extending the life of books, and providing protection from deleterious influences. The project awaits the design and construction of a facility for the DEZ process in the Washington, D.C., area, probably at Fort Dietrick, Maryland.

The Canadian Public Archives and the National Library of Canada are engaged in a similar program, processing books in magnesium carbonate dissolved in a liquefied gas solvent. They are treating 80,000 books annually and may increase this volume with the construction of additional facilities.[12]

11. Ann Russell, "Northeast Document Conservation Center: Case Study in Cooperative Conservation," *The American Archivist* 45 (Winter 1982):48.

12. Richard D. Smith, "Mass Deacidification: The Wei T'o Way," *College and Research Library News* (Dec. 1984):588–93.

8 Insurance and Risk Management

1865. London. . . . By this same fire there was also destroyed the Humboldt Library, consisting of about 17,000 volumes. I fear a good friend of our Association . . . was a heavy loser by this event. A $5,000 policy expired at noon on the very day of the fire, and had not been renewed.[1]

Risk Management

People in the insurance industry describe insurable items in terms of their risk; thus, considered for the likelihood of loss, an item may be a good risk, a bad risk, or anything in between, based on recognized sources of loss and the nature of the controls exercised over them. The science of protecting against and preparing for losses is referred to as "risk management."

Libraries present several loss exposures, including the building and furnishings, the collections, the continuity of operations, and all activities related to the library. Losses from windstorm, fire, flood, injury to an employee or a patron, and collision of a bookmobile can all be protected against through insurance contracts or policies. This is the traditional way of protecting against loss.

Risk management, however, goes well beyond the purchasing of insurance. It provides methods for stabilizing losses, sometimes through insurance contracts but often through establishing reserve funds or other financial devices for making up/paying losses. The risk manager may choose to self-insure for losses up to $500,000, for example, and obtain insurance protection only for levels above that amount, with one company or a number of companies sharing losses in the higher levels (well beyond the normal or predicted range of probable loss).

Loss control is an essential function of risk management. It involves the investment of money and the establishment of specific control measures in order either to reduce the probability of a loss or reduce the extent of a loss. Loss control programs are frequently called safety engineering, loss prevention, fire protection, fire prevention, etc. Whenever the potential for loss exists in any activity or in any property, it is possible to establish a program of loss control

1. Cornelius Walford, "Chronological Sketch of the Destruction of Libraries by Fire" (Manchester, 1879), reprinted in *Managing the Library Fire Risk,* 2nd ed. (Berkeley: Univ. of California, 1979), p. 137.

to reduce that potential, remove hazardous conditions, improve hazardous operations, and lessen the probability of loss-producing incidents. In the library, loss control activities relate to the planning and design of facilities; security programs; problem patron management; fire protection and fire prevention; water damage prevention; and materials preservation and conservation.

The insurance needs of libraries vary according to the size of the library and the nature of the collections. These needs also are affected by the design and construction of the building, and the level of protection it offers against various perils. A few principles apply to all libraries, however. First of all, insurance is not a do-it-yourself project, even for a small library. It is good to obtain the professional services of an established broker or agent who has access to various carriers, and even to seek the occasional advice of another professional to review the program.

Second, it is important to review the insurance schedule frequently, since values tend to increase, which thus requires the readjustment of valuations and coverages to provide adequate protection. Added space, new equipment purchased or leased, new construction, or the acquisition of an important collection are all changes that require readjustments. In a 1981 study of thirty-two incendiary fires that occurred in libraries, only five respondents were satisfied that their insurance coverage was current and adequate at the time fire struck.[2]

Some library experts prescribe a risk management policy statement as the basis for insurance protection for a library. A statement for a small library should be more detailed than one for a large library. The latter presents the opportunity to benefit from competitive bidding, as well as the potential for a large deductible (a self-insurance device for absorbing one's own losses up to a specified percentage of the library's annual budget). Because a large library is often part of a very large university or governmental entity, it is not unusual for it to be carrying a deductible in excess of $1,000,000. But even at this level, the library will be fully insured for losses above the self-insured limit.

Nor is self insurance ruled out for small libraries. It can apply where the risks in any category are small, where the possibility of loss is remote, and where losses are moderate and predictable from year to year. It may not be a good idea to insure against window breakage due to vandalism, for example, if the predictable annual loss would be less than the cost of insurance against such losses.

Very large libraries, typically those in a big city or in a university system, will have an insurance program overseen by a full-time risk manager. A smaller library needs the attention of a dependable agent or broker who is not limited to a single carrier and who can be depended upon to obtain competitive rates. It may be productive also to obtain quotations from interested outside agents or from a professional risk management and insurance consultant, to make sure the agent or broker of record is providing adequate protection at a competitive price. At least once a year, the board should meet to discuss insurance and hear a report prepared by the agent or broker and the librarian, detailing necessary adjustments in agreed upon values, coverages, and carriers.

2. John Morris, "Protecting the Library from Fire," *Library Trends* 33 (Summer, 1984):49–50.

The views of libraries that are held by underwriters of insurance, as shown in *Best's Underwriting Guide,* should also be of interest to risk managers and insurance buyers (see Appendix A).

Loss Exposures

The terms that follow identify the common perils that may be covered by or excluded from the library's property policy. Exclusions are named in the policy separately from the perils that are covered:

> Fire (and lightning).
> Extended coverage: Windstorm, cyclone, tornado, hail. Explosion (except steam boiler). Aircraft and vehicle damage. Smoke damage (from faulty heating plants). Riot, riot attending a strike, and civil commotion.
> Vandalism and malicious mischief.
> Sonic boom.
> Sprinkler leakage.
> Water damage from defective plumbing, heating, and air conditioning systems.
> Collapse of buildings or structures.
> Glass breakage (from other than designated perils).
> Burglary, theft, and robbery.
> Employee dishonesty.
> Steam boiler explosion.
> Transit, including collision or upset.
> Earthquake.
> Flood, backing up of sewers, and surface waters.
> Autos, trucks, and bookmobiles, whether owned, leased, or hired by the library, as well as vehicles owned by others and driven on library business.
> Steam boiler. The standard property policy excludes damage to or caused by steam boilers, so they have to be endorsed on the policy with an extra premium; this entitles the insured library to inspection services for this vessel (and for other pressure vessels, if insured, such as hot water heating boilers). Local or state law requires inspections of large steam boilers, and the carrier's inspection satisfies this need.
> Plate glass. Breakage of plate glass is covered under the extended coverage portion of the fire policy, except for any breakage due to vandalism.
> Property in transit. Books and works of art loaned outside the library are subject to loss. Libraries should check with their insurance person about the need for a transportation floater.
> Extra expense. This coverage will pay for the additional costs of temporarily doing business at another location following a severe fire or other disaster, or for rented facilities of any kind necessitated by such an event.
> Fine arts. Specialized property coverage is available for higher valued art works.

An "all risks" policy will cover some of the above items, but may exclude some also, such as "inherent vice," for example, damage to books from mold, fungus, and various insect infestations.[3]

Tort liability and other library liability arise from damage or injury to persons alleged to be the result of the deliberate or negligent actions of employees or agents, or of a failure in a duty owed the public, such as the following:

Bodily injury to persons (other than employees) who may be injured due to negligence on the part of the insured, such as injury from a fall allegedly caused by a defect in the premises (e.g., a faulty step or sidewalk), or by a wrongful act of some other person.

Personal injury, which includes torts such as false arrest, detention, or imprisonment; or malicious prosecution, libel, slander, defamation, violation of the right to privacy, wrongful entry or eviction, or any other invasion of the right to privacy. This coverage is important in such functions as protecting the library against problem patrons who may say their rights were violated when they were required to show the contents of a bag or to remove outer clothing at the desk when they were leaving.

Civil and constitutional rights violations, such as the rights of women and minorities. Libraries should inquire about coverage or the absence of coverage.

Liability for damage to the property of others. Standard forms exclude coverage for property in the care, custody, or control of the insured (the library), or used or occupied by it.

Contracts in which the library has agreed to hold harmless or indemnify the other party for liability for injuries related to the terms of the contract. Some contractual obligations and maintenance agreements are automatically covered under a standard liability policy; others must be carefully written into the policy with a special endorsement.

Directors' (or trustees') and officers' liability. This covers any liability risk to which the officers are subject and which may not be covered in the standard liability policy.

Other insurable risks:

Injury to employees. Workers' compensation insurance is required of all employers; it provides indemnity for injured employees and protects the employer as well.

Employee dishonesty. Normally this is a fidelity bond, covering all employees (for loss of money or property) without naming the employees, including supervisors and officers.

Loss Reduction and Control

In all insurable areas there are opportunities for loss control as a function of risk management. In the library these are most obvious in preventive mainte-

3. Gerald E. Myers, *Insurance Manual for Libraries* (Chicago: American Library Association, 1977), 2–4.

nance and loss prevention programs, many of which were detailed in the earlier chapters of this book. It should be apparent that if the prevention of all losses were possible, it would not be necessary to carry insurance. The insurance industry recognizes this by offering discounts on fire insurance premiums for libraries that use automatic suppression and detection systems, by offering workers' compensation premium adjustments, and in other ways. *Best's Loss Control Engineering Manual,* a guide for insurance and risk management organizations and for industry generally, devotes several pages to libraries (see Appendix B). The information is sound and can be used in loss control activities and inspections, and as a basis for conversations with the insurer's loss control representative during on-site inspection tours.

Fire Suppression

One loss control device deserves particular mention here—automatic sprinkler systems. A benefit of installing automatic sprinkler systems that is not well known is the possibility of trade-offs with code limitations. For instance, a sprinklered building may be permitted longer travel distance to an exit, fewer exits, and more liberal standards for the burning characteristics of interior finishes and furnishings. Requirements vary somewhat according to the state or municipal rules in effect, but the economies to be realized should be explored with the local authority having jurisdiction over life safety specifications in the design of buildings.

When automatic sprinkler protection is mentioned in relation to libraries, many people immediately respond that "water is worse than fire for books." This platitude appeared in the library literature as long ago as 1870 and is still circulating. In fact, it is the sincere belief of one school of thought that any automatic detection system is preferable to sprinkler protection. This belief is based on the conviction that when a fire is reported by a detection system to a central station, there will be an immediate response by a fire department, and that the firefighters will string a hose line, enter the building, locate the fire, and put water on it, being circumspect about not wetting any book that is not actually burning.

Advocates of sprinklers, notably fire protection engineers, point out that sprinklers would have put water on the fire at the outset, without requiring major intervention and dousing of materials by the fire department. Planners and risk managers should obtain the counsel of fire service officers and fire protection engineers regarding the merits of various systems.

Mobile/Compact Storage

One area in loss control that should not be left to chance is the maintenance and operation of mobile/compact shelving. Safety requires the watchful maintenance of microswitches on flanges designed to prevent the inadvertent crushing of a person between converging shelf units. For this reason, mobile storage is better suited to closed stacks, archives, and lightly used collections than, for example, to periodicals. The experience of one sizable eastern library has confirmed this. Every week a sudden onslaught of junior high school scholars en masse, intent on gathering information from periodicals for writing assignments, creates a kind of frantic game in which compact shelving is constantly in motion at certain hours. Conventional shelving of these materials would relieve wear and tear on mobile shelving and would reduce whatever danger is latent in the heavy use of the system.

Motorized systems have a built-in fire hazard. Fire protection engineers have speculated that the spontaneous occurrence of a fire in such systems is not at all impossible because electric motors are employed, usually one to every shelving unit. As a system ages and as certain units are heavily used, the likelihood of the malfunctioning or overloading of a motor increases. Apart from any consideration of arson, this motor hazard, combined with the formidable fire loading of the shelving units, more than justifies the requirement of automatic fire suppression systems.

Adjusting the Loss

Property loss is adjusted by the insurer either on a replacement basis (assessing the replacement cost without deducting for depreciation) by determining the replacement cost and then deducting for depreciaton. In general, it is prudent to pay the additional premium required for replacement insurance, particularly for buildings, the cost of which tends to increase from year to year rather than go down.

Valuation of the building is established through one of several methods that are fundamentally related to the cost of replacing it at the current labor and materials costs. For furniture and fixtures, a reliable inventory is needed for establishing a total insurable value and for proving a loss. This should be a part of the insurance program before or at the time the insurance policy is written.

Property of others held by the library or for which the library assumes responsibility should also involve a written agreement as to the value of the property in the event of a loss. This will avoid any misunderstanding, embarrassment, or litigation that might arise if a loss occurs without an agreement. Fine arts, rare books, and sculpture should be priced by a curator in the appropriate field in order to insure it properly. By insuring such an item on the "valued" policy form, the carrier accepts the stated value if a claim is made later for the theft or destruction of the item.

Insurance Policies

Maximum credits are usually extended to libraries. A "package policy" will usually be offered, which combines any number of coverages into one and includes a package policy credit that reduces the premium to a figure somewhat below the aggregate of premiums for the individual policies. It may not be the best arrangement, however, so alternative plans should be examined.

It is a good idea for a library to have a "blanket" property policy to bring together a number of locations under one coverage with a single premium. In the event of loss, blanket coverage relieves the library of concern about errors in the valuation of individual locations.

There are three methods of insuring library books and materials. The *blan-*

ket contents form insures the books along with the furniture, fixtures, and equipment at 90 percent coinsurance and with an agreed amount clause, by which the library annually adjusts the valuation of the collections. The *valuable papers* form provides very broad "all risks" coverage, but it has certain disadvantages. Some risk managers believe that the library can have the best of both worlds by using this form and modifying it to cover the replacement cost for items that are actually replaced and providing a single agreed upon amount of insurance on a blanket basis.

The third alternative, the *Hartford library policy,* is a specialized coverage program written only by some insurers. It requires an annual declaration of agreed upon values. These values become the basis of any claim, without regard to the actual value or the replacement value of the individual items that are destroyed. This model policy was developed as a joint project of the American Library Association, Gage-Babcock & Associates, Inc., and the Hartford Fire Insurance Company.[4] It has been used, with modifications, by other insurance carriers. However, it lacks the flexibility of the blanket form, which does not limit the library to a specific value for each book or category of books, nor to a total value for all books and library materials.

Comprehensive and Umbrella Coverages

The comprehensive public liability policy covers the library for most contingencies arising out of ownership of the building and the operations of the library; coverage extends to bodily injury and property damage, including liability for elevators, products (if any), and the operations of independent contractors. Coverage for personal injury, as described earlier, may be added by endorsement, as well as by contractual liability. Judgments made against employees for negligence can be covered with a nominal additional premium charge, and other endorsements are available as well. High limits are important and should be discussed with the library's broker or agent.

Excess liability protects the insured from shock losses above the limits ordinarily considered necessary; for this reason, it is called umbrella liability. It is a broad form of coverage available in multiples of $1,000,000, and it can be effective outside the scope of even those basic policies that require a substantial deductible.

Errors and Omissions Insurance Plan

Small libraries are given special consideration through an Errors and Omissions Insurance Plan sponsored by the American Library Association for its member libraries. The policy provides protection for the library staff, administration, and governing board against the costs of any legal actions taken or judgments made against them based on their library duties. The small library, one that has fewer than twenty-five staff, may insure at a liability limit of $500,000 or $1,000,000. Larger libraries may not insure at the lower limit. The plan has the endorsement of ALA's insurance advisors, but it is administered by an insurance organization that is not under the control of ALA.[5]

4. Edward M. Johnson, ed., *Protecting the Library and Its Resources* (Chicago: American Library Association, 1963), p. 184.

5. For further information, write to the ALA Insurance Plan, Lock Box 1778, Des Moines, IA 50306.

New Construction

An important form of protection when new construction is being undertaken is a performance bond to be obtained from the contractor. Certificates of insurance should also be obtained from the contractor and from subcontractors on essential coverages. The construction contract should include a "hold harmless" or indemnity clause so that any liability for accidents and injuries is transferred to the contractor, since in certain situations the owner (library) might otherwise be held liable.

Action to Take at Times of Injury or Loss

Accidents and other incidents that may result in claims should be reported at the earliest possible time to the insurer, agent, or broker. It is prudent to write a letter as well as make a telephone call for this purpose at once, particularly in any situation in which the insurer needs to make an investigation at the library. Any major property loss, for example, demands a call immediately, as does any injury to a patron. For this reason, the telephone number of the insurance claim person or broker should be near the top of the call list in the emergency and disaster plans.

An incident report should be completed on any incident that occurs on the library premises or that relates to the library and that might develop into a claim against the library. This is true also of incidents that should be brought to the attention of other staff members, even though no claim is made and no injury results. Accidents sometimes occur that do not result in injury but are only a matter of chance; it is also good to consider these to determine if any improvement in the premises or change in operations is needed. An example might be a slip and fall that results when a janitor mops the floor and fails to place a temporary barrier around the wet area to keep people off until the floor has dried. Even if the person is not injured, the incident nevertheless should be recorded and action taken to improve the procedure.

Protecting against Litigation

Librarians are becoming more aware of their legal responsibilities. At the 1986 conference of the Public Library Association, Donald Sager, director of the Milwaukee Public Library, listed some points to be considered.[6] After pointing out that libraries can be sued for investment losses, personal injury, and issues of intellectual freedom, he presented this battery of defenses against likely sources of lawsuits: Put an indemnification statement in the library bylaws, using the American Library Trustee Association (ALTA) model. Get a letter from your city or county legal counsel specifying services, buy all the insurance you can afford, bond any employee who handles funds, get a management letter with your annual audits, and change auditors frequenty. Check your current book selection, personnel, and other policies with legal counsel. Demand custodial repair for staff and patron safety, insist on excellence in management, and walk the branches and the central library often.

6. *American Libraries* 17 (May, 1986):322.

Appendix A
Best's Underwriting Guide (Libraries)

sic code 8231 Libraries and Information Centers

Line	Best's Hazard Index	Underwriting Comments
Automobile Liability	2	Higher if bookmobile used.
General Liability	6	Increases as level of community use increases.
Product Liability — Completed Operations	1	Higher if operation includes food service.
Workers' Compensation	3	Higher for employees other than professional or clerical.
Crime	5	Higher if there are many rare books and documents.
Fire and E. C.	6	Low frequency but potential for high severity.
Business Interruption	3	
Inland Marine	5	

Low 1-3, Medium 4-6, High 7-9, Very High 10

Related Classifications

Art Galleries/Dealers

Bookbinding

Book Stores — New and Used — Retail

Colleges and Universities

Movie Theatres — Indoor

Museums

Printing — Quick Printers

Schools — Elementary and Secondary —

Private and Public

Special Exposures

Water damage to books and materials

Damage to or theft of rare books, fine arts

Arson

Bookmobiles

RISK DESCRIPTION

Libraries acquire, maintain, catalog, index and file books, periodicals, tapes, microfilms and records, which are available for loan, copy or reference. Typewriters, cameras, video recorders and microcomputers may be available for loan or rent. Increased emphasis is being placed on audio and visual media usage and automation of information systems. Many libraries belong to a computer network for information sharing.

Some libraries display and loan works of art, show films, and provide a variety of speakers or workshops for adults and children. The library may provide space for community organizations to conduct activities.

A large library may have repair facilities similar to a book bindery; a print shop; a conservation department (where materials are cleaned, repaired, laminated, encapsulated in plastic film and deacidified); an auditorium; and food service.

Many communities operate mobile units with the interior adapted to accommodate library facilities. These bookmobiles travel a regular route. Some libraries have branches, which offer services on a reduced scale.

The library may be publicly owned or part of a private collection or owned by a business, scientific, cultural or religious organization. The stacks may be open to the public or closed. Library buildings, which may be owned or leased, cover a wide range of architectural styles and types of construction. Large undivided areas, high ceilings, concealed spaces, vertical openings between levels, and complicated exit patterns can be found in many libraries. In some libraries, self-supporting multistory book stacks are used. The building is actually a shell; floors are metal platforms built around the stacks. This type of bookstack has slotlike vertical openings between the stairs and walkways.

High-density mobile shelving systems mounted on tracks are being used to save space in many libraries. These systems are an application of modern warehousing technology.

Copyright 1984 by A. M. Best Company, Inc. Reprinted by permission.

MATERIALS AND EQUIPMENT

Books, periodicals, records, tapes, films, slides, microfilms and microfiche, discs, photographs, documents, works of art; card catalog and shelf list.

Office machines, minicomputers, audio and visual equipment, duplicators, microfilm readers and printers.

Shelving (wood or metal); high-density mobile shelving systems; cabinets; media storage systems; book trucks, rolling tables; ladders, step stools; carrels, tables and chairs; book returns; exhibit cases; book conveyor systems.

Paper cutters, stapling machines, laminators, binding machines; spray and liquid adhesives, book lacquer, laminating material (cellulose acetate), protective polyester film, organic solvents, deacidifying solutions (spray or liquid); insecticides, fumigants.

Kitchen equipment and supplies.

Automobile Liability

Many libraries have one or more trucks or cars for general work and transportation of supplies and books.

If a bookmobile is used, its age and condition are important. Where is it driven? How long is the route? Have advance arrangements been made concerning where the bookmobile will be parked at outreach sites?

A non-owned automobile exposure is likely if employees do off-premises work — i.e., delivering books to shut-ins, doing library work in prisons or convalescent centers, or conducting workshops.

See also Basic Insurance Facts — Automobile Liability.

General Liability

Slips and falls may occur on slippery floors or uneven walking surfaces, or off wheeled step stools or movable stepladders. Many older buildings have additions accessible by ramps or steps. The stairs may lack handrails, or rails may not be securely attached. Patrons may be injured by books falling off high shelves. Broken or cracked glass display cases and poorly maintained chairs and tables may be sources of injury. High-density mobile shelving systems that can be controlled by patrons must have an adequate safety interlock system so that no one can be trapped or crushed within the stacks.

Consider planning for life safety in an emergency: clearly marked exit routes in the stacks, lighted signs over exits, emergency lighting and a public address system. (See NFPA Life Safety Code #101.) Required exit doors sometimes are padlocked and chained to thwart vandals or prevent thefts, particularly in libraries with high-value collections or in college libraries. Electromechanical or electromagnetic locking systems on doors are permitted if they afford equivalent life safety. Have the needs of the handicapped been considered?

Is safe capacity posted in auditoriums and is occupancy restricted accordingly?

The number of disturbed and destitute people who visit libraries has been increasing, especially in urban areas. Procedures for handling the "problem patron" should exist so that other patrons can be protected without the library incurring suits for false arrest or some other charge brought by the problem patron. Libraries should have close contact with local police departments; professional security personnel on the premises might be desirable in some situations.

Libraries that provide many programs for children and adults, allow community organizations to use the facilities, and utilize volunteers who may be teenagers or senior citizens will have a greater general liability exposure.

If the library has a bookmobile, pay particular attention to the walking surfaces within it and the steps leading into it. Are sturdy handrails provided?

Product Liability and Completed Operations

There is little or no exposure here. See Restaurants or Catering if the library provides a food service or serves food at receptions.

Directors' and Officers' Liability

Although library trustees have not been the target of lawsuits, the trend of the courts has been to place heavy responsibility for proper performance upon directors and trustees in general.

Professional Liability (Errors and Omissions)

For public libraries, Public Officials and Employees Liability insurance is available as a surplus coverage. The forms of coverage vary widely among insurance companies and may include protection for the Board of Directors as well as employees, part-time employees and trustees. The claims covered may include censorship liability, sex and civil rights discrimination to the extent allowed by law, and negligent misappropriations, among others.

Workers' Compensation

Frequent causes of loss are back strains and hernias brought about by lifting piles or boxes of books, injuries due to falls from movable ladders or step stools, injuries from collapsing shelving, and cuts from sharp instruments used to open cartons. Sturdy, properly anchored ladders and good housekeeping are necessary to minimize losses.

Mechanical book conveyor systems and mobile storage systems are potential sources of pinch or crush-type injuries. Electrical interlocks to stop the equipment before an injury can take place are necessary to control the danger.

With an increase in the number of disturbed or problem patrons in libraries, employees are exposed to physical injury at the hands of a patron. Especially in urban areas, library security and staff training to deal with problem patrons are important. Is police back-up readily available? A professional security staff might be desirable.

Workers in the conservation department use paper-cutting machines, laminators that employ heat and pressure to seal documents in a protective covering, organic solvents for cleaning, and spray adhesives. Fumigants and insecticides are used periodically. In libraries where a deacidification process is used, employees dip materials in or spray them with a solution that reduces acid and an alcohol solvent and trichlorotrifluoroethane. If spray booths and exhaust hoods are not available, employees must wear a respirator and goggles.

Refer to the appropriate write-up for hazards associated with building maintenance, binding or printing.

Employees are exposed to vehicular accidents while driving

bookmobiles and traveling to off-premises tasks. Work in prisons or isolated areas may expose workers to additional hazards.

See also Basic Insurance Facts — Workers' Compensation.

Crime

Valuable collections, rare books and documents, office equipment and audiovisual equipment are targets of theft. University libraries are at greater risk. To decrease the book theft hazard, electronic devices that signal a guard if a book is being removed without being checked out can be installed. Are valuable collections isolated and is access to them restricted and monitored? Is a burglar alarm system in force? Does the library have a direct communication link with the police?

A theft of valuable property may result from employee collusion with outsiders. Employees also may join with suppliers to defraud the library. Pre-employment checks should be made on all employees. The cash exposure, however, will be slight, especially if frequent bank deposits are made.

Fire and E.C.

Although with less frequency than in mercantile or manufacturing occupancies, fires do occur in libraries with considerable regularity and can cause severe losses. Leading causes of fires in this class are incendiarism, malfunction of heating equipment, defective or inadequate electrical equipment (including the use of small-gauge extension cords), careless smoking, contractors' operations (especially welding and cutting), spontaneous ignition of oily rags, and exposures from adjacent occupancies.

The high fuel loading in book stacks and media storage areas, particularly in high-density storage systems, could result in fire intensity and duration similar to those possible in warehouse occupancies. Values are substantial; in some cases contents are irreplaceable. Although most libraries are of fire-resistive construction, serious damage has occurred in fire-resistive as well as combustible construction. Without prompt detection of fire, transmission of an alarm, and availability of internal suppression, construction materials alone will not guarantee superior protection of the contents. Some libraries are in old, converted buildings, where the problems may be magnified.

Compartmentation of the building is essential to limit destruction to a single area. This compartmentation should be achieved by fire-resistive wall and floor construction, openings protected by self-closing fire doors, enclosed stairways, protected vertical openings, and air-handling systems designed to prevent the passage of smoke, heat and fire. Boilers and furnaces in particular should be cut off from the remainder of the structure.

Towers and windowless areas present problems with fire-fighting access and smoke removal. Roof ventilation, knockout panels, emergency lighting and automatic fire-suppression systems are desirable in such areas.

Sheet steel shelves are preferable to either wood or U-bar shelves; metal book trucks are preferable to wood. Are there interior finishes and furnishings that would increase the fire hazard?

Casual vandalism by teenagers is responsible for a growing number of incendiary fires. Because arsonists usually strike when the library is closed, the first line of defense is preventing people from breaking in at night or hiding out in the building after closing. Often, the design of the library building and the layout of the grounds are serious handicaps in preventing vandalism and break-ins. Clear space around the library and perimeter lighting are helpful where the risk of vandalism is high. Book drops leading to the interior of the building are very vulnerable to arsonists. Three ways to deal with this hazard are (1) to use freestanding book drops outside the library, (2) to use fire-resistive metal book carts to receive drop materials, or (3) to reinforce book drops and mail slots with fire-resistive materials to prevent fire spread. Because a set fire may flash almost immediately, a high risk of arson in a given area puts a premium on automatic extinguishing.

Although often resisted because of the possibility of water damage, automatic sprinklers are desirable because they can confine a fire to a small area. Experience with sprinklers in libraries has been good. In addition, sprinkler systems that minimize water damage are available: hydraulically calculated systems, water fog sprinkler heads, stop-and-go-systems, and cross-zoned detection systems that require impulses from two well-separated circuits to trigger the system, preventing premature action. At the least, libraries can utilize spot sprinklers in such high-hazard areas as janitors' closets and in areas containing substantial combustible contents. Halon 1301 is the agent of choice for protecting locations where values are high and can be confined to a compact space, and where water damage might create a severe salvage problem.

Water damage caused by broken water and steam pipes, water entering the building during construction, condensate, seepage, storm-driven rain, a leaking roof, faulty drains and sewers, and flooding is a serious threat to libraries. Water-damage disasters related to fire fighting, however, have occurred only in libraries not protected with sprinklers. Water-damaged materials can be restored by vacuum drying or freeze drying, but such restoration generally is economical only for irreplaceable items. The Library of Congress publication "Salvage of Water-Damaged Library Materials" details the procedures but states, "Replacement is nearly always cheaper than restoration." Therefore, the library should have a list of which materials can be replaced and which should be reclaimed or restored in the event of a disaster. Salvage procedures — the use of salvage covers for books, plans for immediate removal or relocation of high-value items, the location of labor and materials resources — should be preplanned for fire and water emergencies. Swift action must be taken if damaged books are to be restored. The entire operation for salvage of books and documents involving freezing, storing, shipping, drying, cleaning, rebinding and reprocessing materials is time-consuming and expensive.

A duplicate copy of the shelf list must be stored at another location; it provides proof of loss and is a guide in replacing books and materials. All important records, especially those on magnetic tapes and discs, should be duplicated and the copies stored at a detached, protected location.

See also Basic Insurance Facts — Fire and E.C.

Business Interruption

Temporary relocation may involve extra expense. Frequently, however, a church or school will donate space. Loss of income is minimal because nearly all libraries are operated on a nonprofit basis.

Larger libraries or systems with extensive EDP equipment may require Extra Expense insurance to cover rental charges for similar equipment. How long would it take to repair or replace damaged equipment? Is substitute equipment available in the event of loss or breakdown of the library's installations?

After a severe loss in a large library, several months to a year could elapse before the library is back to full service. Books in a technical library may take longer to replace than ordinary books, thus extending the period of interruption.

Inland Marine

Consideration must be given to the scheduling of rare books and manuscripts, special collections, fine arts and bookmobile contents. A fire detection and suppression system is strongly recommended for libraries that house irreplaceable books and works of art. Are high-value items confined to a well-guarded area? Are the premises patrolled regularly?

When fine arts are borrowed by a library for an exhibit, it is customary for that library to secure and pay for insurance to and from the premises and during the exhibition. Such bailee coverage must be written with care because the values may be extremely high.

Special coverage also may be necessary for EDP equipment. In addition, a floater policy commonly is used to insure such items as cameras and projection equipment.

Are bookmobiles parked away from the library premises overnight? How are the contents protected?

> **A physical survey report and an analysis of prior losses are necessary to underwrite this class.**

Underwriter's Check List

Does the library have high-value rare books, documents and works of art?

Are valuable collections segregated and is access to them monitored?

What is the construction of the book shelves?

Is the building compartmentalized?

Is the heating system in a cut-off area?

Is prohibition of smoking enforced?

Does the library have an automatic sprinkler system?

Has vandalism been a problem?

Are important records duplicated and are the duplicates stored safely off the premises?

Does the library have a bookmobile?

Appendix B
Best's Loss Control Engineering Manual (Libraries)

Line	Best's Hazard Index*	Line	Best's Hazard Index*
Automobile Liability	2(a)	Crime	5(e)
General Liability	6(b)	Fire and E.C.	6
Product Liability — Completed Operations	1(c)	Business Interruption	3
Workers' Compensation	3(d)	Inland Marine	5

*Low 1-3, Medium 4-6, High 7-9, Very High 10

(a) Higher if bookmobile used.
(b) Increases as level of use increases.
(c) Higher if operation includes food service.
(d) Higher if other than professional or clerical.
(e) Higher if many rare books and documents.

SIC 8231

Related Classifications

Art Galleries/Dealers
Bookbinding
Book Stores
Colleges and Universities
Movie Theatres — Indoor
Museums
Printing — Quick Printers
Schools — Elementary and Secondary

DESCRIPTION

Libraries acquire, maintain, catalog, index and file books, periodicals, tapes, microfilms and records, which are available for loan, copy or reference. Typewriters, cameras, video recorders and microcomputers may be available for loan or rent. Increased emphasis is being placed on audio and visual media usage and automation of information systems. Many libraries belong to a computer network for information sharing.

Some libraries display and loan works of art, show films, and provide a variety of speakers or workshops for adults and children. The library may provide space for community organizations to conduct activities.

A large library may have repair facilities similar to a book bindery; a print shop; a conservation department (where materials are cleaned, repaired, laminated, encapsulated in plastic film and deacidified); an auditorium; and food service.

Many communities operate mobile units with the interior adapted to accommodate library facilities. These bookmobiles travel a regular route. Some libraries have branches which offer services on a reduced scale.

The library may be publicly owned or part of a private collection or owned by a business, scientific, cultural or religious organization. The stacks may be open to the public or closed. Library buildings cover a wide range of architectural styles and types of construction. Large undivided areas, high ceilings, concealed spaces, vertical openings between levels, and complicated exit patterns can be found in many libraries. In some libraries, self-supporting multistory book stacks are used. The building is actually a shell; floors are metal platforms built around the stacks. This type of book stack has slotlike vertical openings between the stairs and walkways.

High-density mobile shelving systems mounted on tracks are being used to save space in many libraries. These systems are an application of modern warehousing technology.

MATERIALS AND EQUIPMENT

Books, periodicals, records, tapes, films, slides, microfilms and microfiche, discs, photographs, documents, works of art; card catalog and shelf list.

Office machines, minicomputers, audio and visual equipment, duplicators, microfilm readers and printers.

Shelving (wood or metal); high-density mobile shelving systems; cabinets; media storage systems; book trucks, rolling tables; ladders, step stools; carrels, tables and chairs; book return receptacles; exhibit cases; book conveyor systems.

Paper cutters, stapling machines, laminators, binding machines; spray and liquid adhesives, book lacquer, laminating material (cellulose acetate), protective polyester film, organic solvents, deacidifying solutions (spray or liquid); insecticides, fumigants.

Kitchen equipment and supplies.

——— EXPOSURES AND CONTROLS ———

AUTOMOBILE LIABILITY

Exposures: Transportation of supplies and books. Bookmobiles; long routes.

On-site Inspection	Items to Investigate
Type, age and condition of vehicles Steps, railings, access arrangement for bookmobile	Experience and age of drivers Use of vehicles — frequency; distances traveled and hazards of the routes Use of employee-owned vehicles for off-premises work (i.e., delivering books to shut-ins or others, conducting workshops); insurance coverage Advance arrangement for parking a bookmobile for safe access by the public Maintenance program for vehicles

FIRE AND E.C.

Exposures: Old buildings, dry wood, highly varnished or waxed surfaces. Large open spaces, high ceilings or dropped ceilings with concealed spaces, open stairways. Narrow aisles; wooden shelves; high loading in book stacks and high-density storage systems. Towers and windowless areas making fire fighting access and smoke removal difficult. Accumulations of furniture and odds and ends in basements or attics. Inadequate wiring and heating systems. Valuable contents, sometimes of very high value or even irreplaceable, but always combustible and vulnerable to water damage. Resistance of library officials to automatic sprinkler systems. (Water-damage disasters related to fire fighting have occurred mostly in libraries *not* protected with sprinklers. The Library of Congress publication "Salvage of Water-Damaged Library Materials" details restoration procedures but states, "Replacement is nearly always cheaper than restoration.") Vandalism and incendiary fires.

On-site Inspection

Construction — combustible; insulation; roof; concealed spaces; alterations

Layout and compartmentation of the building — fire-resistive walls and floors; openings protected by self-closing fire doors; enclosed stairways; protected vertical openings; air-handling systems designed to prevent passage of smoke, heat and fire

Condition and location of heating system — Is it in a cut-off fire-resistive area?

Condition and adequacy of electrical system and wiring

Attic and basement storage

Accessibility to fire-fighting equipment

Any interior finishes or furnishings that would increase the fire hazard

Heat and smoke alarm systems

Automatic sprinkler systems — Are they controlled to use no more water than necessary to extinguish a fire? Where valuable contents would be irreparably damaged by water, are special fixed systems with other extinguishing agents utilized?

Adequate portable fire extinguishers

Lightning arresters

Type of book drops — If they are not freestanding outside, are the book receptacles reinforced with fire-resistive material or otherwise protected?

Condition of water or steam pipes, roof, drains and sewers that serve the library — any indications of previous water damage

Hazards of adjacent occupancies or properties — amount of clear space around the facility; perimeter lighting

Items to Investigate

Maintenance program for electrical, air conditioning and heating, fire suppression and detection systems

Record of boiler inspections; date of last inspection and carrier

Repair work, binding, use of solvents and other fire prevention problems

Daily disposal of refuse outside of building

Restriction of smoking

Emergency preplans — Are all employees instructed in the proper action to take? What procedures have been planned for safeguarding or moving important books or collections, including swift action for salvaging?

List of which materials can be replaced and which should be reclaimed or restored in the event of a disaster so quick action can be taken — Is there a duplicate record at another safe location?

Adequacy of public fire protection and water supply; response time — Have emergency plans been discussed with the fire department?

Cost of restoring irreplaceable water-damaged books and other items

Record of vandalism incidents in the area and in the library

Refer also to NFPA 910, Recommended Practices for Protection of Libraries and Library Collections

GENERAL LIABILITY

Exposures: Slippery or uneven floors, walking surfaces and parking lot; snow and ice; poor lighting. Worn or torn floor coverings. Stairs and ramps lacking handrails or with loose handrails improperly attached to walls or too low. Broken, cracked or sharp edges on glass display cases. Tables or chairs in disrepair. Improperly stacked books; weak book racks; high density mobile shelving systems controlled by patrons. Elevators. Required exit doors sometimes are padlocked and chained. Handling of disruptive patrons.

On-site Inspection

Condition of floors and floor coverings, walking surfaces and parking lot

Condition of stairs and ramps — Are there adequate handrails, firmly secured?

Provisions for the handicapped

Condition and strength of furniture

Adequacy of lighting in book aisles, walkways and parking lot

Condition of glass display cases

Safely stacked books in sturdy secured racks — high-density mobile shelving that can be controlled by patrons equipped with safety interlock system

Clearly marked exit routes in the stack areas, emergency lighting available and public address system

Adequate exits and fire escapes, clearly marked and lighted; compliance with NFPA Life Safety Code #101

Bookmobile walking surfaces and steps leading into it — Are sturdy handrails provided?

Items to Investigate

Maintenance program for care, inspection and repair of furniture, elevators, floors, racks and premises inside and out

Arrangements for prompt removal of snow and ice

Procedures for handling the "problem patron" — Are employees instructed in how to handle disruptive, disturbed or destitute people who visit the facility? Is there a good working relationship with the municipal police department if assistance is needed?

Any professional security personnel employed — Are they trained regarding their legal powers and restrictions?

Type of programs provided for children and adults; frequency

Use of the facilities by community or civic organizations for special meetings, programs or exhibits — Have any events been of a controversial nature that caused disruptive demonstrations?

Is occupancy of auditoriums or other meeting areas restricted to the safe capacity regulations? How is it controlled?

PRODUCT LIABILITY AND COMPLETED OPERATIONS

Exposures: Little or no exposure here. See Restaurants or Catering if the library provides a food service or serves food at receptions.

WORKERS' COMPENSATION

Exposures: Handling, moving and lifting books and materials. Opening cartons; sharp tools. Using ladders and stools for reaching shelves; unsturdy shelving. Mechanical book conveyor systems and mobile storage systems with a potential for pinch or crush-type injuries. Possibility of physical injury at the hands of disturbed or problem patrons, especially in urban areas. Vehicular accidents while driving bookmobiles and traveling to tasks off-premises, such as service to prisons or isolated regions. Workers in the conservation department use paper-cutting machines, laminators that employ heat and pressure to seal documents in a protective covering, organic solvents for cleaning, and spray adhesives. Fumigants and insecticides used periodically. Maintenance staff has janitorial exposure. Refer to the appropriate classification if there is a print shop, bindery or food service. See also General Liability.

On-site Inspection

Housekeeping — uncluttered aisles and work areas
Adequacy of lighting
Non-skid stools or ladders properly anchored and in good repair
Condition and sturdiness of book stacks — mechanical book conveyor and mobile storage systems equipped with safety interlocks
Sheathed cutting tools
Is there a security staff on duty?

Items to Investigate

Supervision and training of employees in safe lifting practices, climbing, proper use of sharp instruments, other materials and equipment involved with the work
Is the staff instructed in safe methods to deal with "problem patrons"? — Is the police department readily available to assist if necessary?
Proportion of part-time, casual or volunteer workers
Amount and type of conservation and repair work performed
Involvement with deacidification treatment of items for preservation before encapsulation or lamination; methods and solutions used — If spray booths and exhaust hoods are not available, do employees wear respirators and goggles?
Precautions taken when fumigants or insecticides are applied
Outreach services provided — hazards of areas and places visited; frequency (See also Automobile Liability.)

CRIME

Exposures: Rare books and documents or fine arts. Office and audiovisual equipment. Employee collusion with outsiders. Slight cash exposure.

On-site Inspection	Items to Investigate
Quantity of rare books, documents, or fine arts Access of public to book stacks, especially in the rare book section Are valuable collections isolated and is access restricted and monitored? Safeguards — electronic devices; burglar alarm system; guard service Records of office audiovisual equipment — identifying marks and numbers, and locations	Screening of employees; reference checks made Maximum value of rare books, documents or fine arts kept at any one time Purchasing, inventory and accounting controls Control of cash receipts for overdue books, duplicating machines or other services Frequency and transportation of bank deposits Hours open to the public

BUSINESS INTERRUPTION

Exposures: Loss of income is minimal because nearly all libraries are operated on a nonprofit basis. Temporary relocation may involve extra expense, as would systems with extensive EDP equipment to cover rental charges of similar equipment. A technical library poses a more serious book replacement problem which may extend the period of interruption.

On-site Inspection	Items to Investigate
	Availability of a substitute location Time required to rebuild Availability of replacement books Dependency on EDP system — availability of substitute equipment; time required to repair or replace damaged equipment; cost of renting similar equipment

INLAND MARINE

Exposures: Rare books and manuscripts, special collections, photographs, paintings, sculpture and other fine arts (see also Art Galeries/Dealers and Museums). Special exhibitions, borrowed fine arts. Bookmobile contents. Water damage. (Vacuum drying and freeze drying have proven to be effective methods of restoration for waterlogged books and papers.) EDP equipment; cameras and projectors; audiovisual equipment.

On-site Inspection

Display of valuables confined to one area or spread throughout the facility

Adequacy of fire protection and security measures for valuables and equipment covered

Are complete inventory records kept up to date?

Items to Investigate

Quantity of fine arts housed or stored on the premises

Accepted value of items covered

Practice of borrowing or lending fine arts for special events — Do loan agreements require borrowers to provide insurance?

Frequency of police patrols

Record of theft or vandalism in the library and in the area

Contents of bookmobiles — Where are they parked overnight?

REFERENCES

OSHA Standards: (Pertinent OSHA standards that apply to this classification; for other appropriate general OSHA standards, see the Introduction, page IX.)

1910.25	Portable Wood Ladders
1910.26	Portable Metal Ladders
1910.176	Handling Materials — General

Glossary

American National Standards Institute (ANSI) coordinates and administers the federated voluntary standardization system in the United States, providing national consensus standards for consumer and worker protection.

amortize To put money aside in order to pay off a debt or to finance an improvement.

arson Willful destruction of property by fire, sometimes to collect money in an insurance fraud.

atrium An open court or hall in a building, usually extending to the roof and sometimes open to the various floor levels.

BAMBAM *Bookline Alert: Missing Books and Manuscripts;* a computer system for recording information about missing and stolen items.

BOCA Building Officials Conference of America is one of four organizations known for model building codes.

CCTV Closed circuit television is a system used for security, in which a number of cameras can transmit to a central monitoring station; a single security person can see what is happening in several places at the same time.

central station A continuously staffed watch station for receiving alarms from automatic suppression and detection systems, typically miles away from the protected property.

cryogenics The science of producing and studying the effects of very low temperatures.

deadbolt lock A springless lock with a bolt moved only by a key from outside or a knob from inside the door; a double-cylinder deadlock requires a key from either side and gives better protection.

decision tree A diagram graphically demonstrating a problem, with lines drawn to show relationships of various alternatives in meeting objectives.

deductible The amount payable by the insured in any loss before any contribution by the insurance carrier.

DEZ Diethyl zinc, used in deacidification of books.

electrolysis Deterioration of metal due to passage through it of a continuous electric current.

electromagnet A magnet depending for its holding power on a continuous electric current.

ESFR Early suppression, fast response; a term applied to a certain class of automatic sprinkler devices and systems.

extrapolate To infer conclusions in one area based on data developed in another area on the premise that the same or similar results can be expected.

fidelity bond An insurance contract that reimburses the employer for a loss resulting from the dishonesty of an employee.

fire resistive construction A term applied to a building designed or built to resist destruction by fire by incorporating such features as protection of steel structural members with masonry to prevent deformation in a severe fire.

fire service The fire department; in the United Kingdom, the fire brigade.

flammable Igniting easily and burning rapidly; in the United Kingdom, inflammable.

fluorescence The property of producing light when acted upon by radiant energy, such as ultraviolet light.

foil A metallic tape used on glass in a burglar alarm system.

Formalin A solution of formaldehyde in water, 37 to 50 percent by volume.

graffiti Drawings or inscriptions crudely drawn in public places.

Halon 1211 Bromochlorodifluormethane ($CBrClF_2$); a gaseous, somewhat toxic extinguishant.

Halon 1301 Bromotrifluormethane ($CBrF_3$); the least toxic of gaseous extinguishants, and the only one approved for occupied spaces.

Halons Halogenated extinguishing agents; hydrocarbons in which one or more hydrogen atoms have been replaced by halogen atoms, thus changing a flammable substance into one that extinguishes fire.

hold harmless A clause in a contract by which one party to the contract is excepted from certain specifically named obligations and transfers these obligations to the other party.

HVAC Heating, ventilating and air conditioning (systems).

in flagrante delicto In the very act of committing an offense.

incendiarism The act of willfully destroying property by fire.

infrared Invisible rays that are just beyond the red end of the spectrum.

inherent vice A term used in insurance to describe a defect or cause of loss arising out of the nature of the material concerned.

intumescent Capable of swelling; a term used to describe the blistering action of certain fire retardant paints.

ionization detector A detection device which sends an alarm when smoke particles interfere with the passage of electric current through an ionized atmosphere.

liability Any legally enforceable obligation.

Life Safety Code A standard (known also as NFPA 101) published by the National Fire Protection Association, widely used and adopted by reference in many jurisdictions as the criterion for life safety in the design of buildings.

loss control A program of measures taken to reduce the possibility of accident, injury, fire, or other loss producing event.

makeup air Air that replaces in equal amount the air drawn out of a room by a heating or ventilating system.

mildew A thin, whitish, furry coating or discoloration produced in damp environments on organic material by fungi.

modular (a) A building design in which floors above the lowest level are supported by a series of columns rather than by fixed, load-bearing walls; (b) a system composed of units of standard measure, but capable of shifting into various arrangements.

negligence Failure to use that degree of care which an ordinary person of reasonable prudence would use.

NFPA The National Fire Protection Association, publisher of the National Fire Codes, a prolific source of information on fire, fire protection and all related topics. In England, the Fire Protection Association (FPA) provides these services.

pallet A low, portable platform used in warehousing.

pan-tilt Action of a TV camera capable of horizontal and vertical movement.

panic hardware An arrangement for releasing the latch on a required exit door when pressure is applied against a horizontal bar across the door.

performance bond A contract guaranteeing that the contractor will do the work in accordance with the terms agreed upon and in the time specified.

photoelectric Depending for operation on the effect of light.

P.O.C. detector A sensing device that alarms in response to visible (smoke) or invisible products of combustion (P.O.C.).

polycarbonate A class of resins that are thermoplastic, tough, transparent, and non-toxic.

proprietary system A protective signaling system serving one or more properties under one ownership; similar in function to a central station system but operated by the owner.

rate-of-rise The term used to describe a thermal detector which is sensitive to the rapid rise of temperature in a fire.

recycling system A suppression system that shuts down if the fire is under control but resumes action if the fire rekindles.

remote system A protective signaling system using leased telephone lines to carry signals to a remote station, such as a fire station or a police station. It requires a separate receiver for each function being monitored, such as waterflow alarm, fire alarm, etc.

R.H. Relative humidity; the amount of moisture in the air relative to the maximum amount the air could contain at the same temperature, expressed as a percentage.

risk manager An officer of the organization who protects it from predictable losses (a) through intelligent control measures to reduce the possibility of loss, and (b) through insurance or other strategies to pay any losses sustained.

sensor A device for sensing and reporting through an automatic system information on fire, water, smoke, intrusion, etc., or whatever it is designed to detect.

spontaneous ignition   The term applied to a fire caused by the heating of a combustible material until it bursts into flame. It results from a combination of air supply and confinement favorable to building up heat faster than it can be dissipated.

standpipe riser   A large-diameter pipe rising vertically through a building to supply water to fire hose connections on the upper floors.

strike plate   The metal plate on a door jamb into which the bolt or latch fits when the door is closed. Sometimes also called strike.

sublimate   To cause water to pass directly from the frozen state into vapor without entering the liquid state.

sump   A pit built into a basement floor to collect casual water.

sump pump   A pump installed permanently in or above a sump and designed to act automatically to remove water from it.

systems approach   As related to fire protection in building design, consideration of fire safety in concert with other subsystems such as electrical, mechanical, etc., and use of engineering technology and methodology.

torr   A unit of pressure equal to 1,333.22 millibars, enough to support a column of mercury one millimeter high under standard conditions.

tort   A violation of a duty of care owed a person, such as might cause injury to one through the (alleged) negligence of another.

trap   A burglar alarm device that signals movement of a door or window.

U.L.   Underwriters Laboratories, Northbrook; a testing laboratory for equipment used in various areas including electrical devices, fire protection, security protection, and fire resistance.

ultrasonic   Having a sound frequency of more than 20,000 vibrations per second, above the range audible to the human ear.

ultraviolet   Lying beyond the violet end of the spectrum; having a wavelength shorter than (approximately) 4000 angstroms.

Uniform Building Code   UBC, a widely used model code, the code of the International Conference of Building Officials.

vermin   Insect pests, commonly lice, mites, fleas.

vidicon   A television camera pickup tube of high sensitivity.

water table   The level below which the ground is saturated with water.

waterflow alarm   A device that sends a signal to a monitoring station when water moves through pipes in the sprinkler system.

Wei T'o   The registered trademark of a nonaqueous book deacidification system. The name is the same as that of an ancient Chinese god that protects books against destruction from fire, worms and insects, and robbers, big or small.

Bibliography

General

BOHEM, HILDA, ed. *Disaster Prevention and Disaster Preparedness.* Berkeley: Univ. of California Press, 1978.

BUCHANAN, SALLY. "Disaster, Prevention, Preparedness and Action." *Library Trends,* 30 (Fall 1981):241–52.

GOETZ, A. H. "Books in Peril: A History of Horrid Catastrophes." *Wilson Library Bulletin,* 47 (Jan. 1973):428–39.

HUNTER, JOHN E. *Emergency Preparedness for Museums, Historic Sites and Archives: An Annotated Bibliography.* Lincoln, Neb.: National Park Service, 1981.

JOHNSON, EDWARD M., ed. *Protecting the Library and Its Resources.* Chicago: American Library Assn., 1963.

O'CONNELL, MILDRED. "Disaster Planning: Writing and Implementing Plans for Collections-Holding Institutions." *Technology and Conservation,* 8 (Summer 1983):18–24.

SABLE, MARTIN H. "The Protection of the Library and Archive: An International Bibliography." *Library and Archival Security,* 5 (Summer/Fall 1983).

SURRENCY, ERWIN. "Guarding Against Disaster." *Law Library Journal,* 66 (Nov. 1973):419–28.

WATERS, PETER. "Disasters Revisited." In *Disasters, Prevention and Coping,* pp. 6–12. Stanford, Calif.: Stanford Univ. Libraries, 1981.

WEBER, DAVID C. "The Vulnerability of Graphic Artifacts." In *Disasters, Prevention and Coping,* pp. 2–5. Stanford, Calif.: Stanford Univ. Libraries, 1981.

Basic Building Security

BRAND, MARVINE. "Security of Academic Library Buildings." *Library and Archival Security,* 3 (Spring 1980):39–47.

FENELLY, LAURENCE J. *Museum, Archival and Library Security.* Boston and London: Butterworths, 1983.

HOLT, RAYMOND M. "Where Security Begins." *Library and Archival Security,* 3 (Fall/Winter 1980):115–23.

O'NEIL, JAMES W. "Strengthen Your Security Posture." *Library Security Newsletter,* 1 (Mar. 1975):1, 7–9.

SAGER, DONALD J. "Protecting the Library After Hours." *Library Journal,* 94 (Oct. 1969):3609–14.

ZAHN, VICTOR R. "Security Alarm Selection for Libraries." *Library Security Newsletter,* 1 (July 1975):1–5.

Problem Patrons

BROWN, MARION, et al. *Problem Patron Manual.* Schenectady: Schenectady County Public Library, 1981.

DELPH, EDWARD W. "Preventing Public Sex in Library Settings." *Library and Archival Security,* 3 (Fall/Winter 1980):29–38.

O'NEIL, JAMES W. "Staff and Patron Safety—8 Most Common Problems." *Library Security Newsletter,* 1 (Sept./Oct. 1975):3–5.

SAGER, DONALD J. "Vandalism in Libraries." *Encyclopedia of Library and Information Science.* Vol. 32. New York: Dekker, 1981.

SUTTON, FRED. "Birmingham Libraries Have Been Facing Quite a Different Crisis: Teenage Gang Hooliganism." *Library Association Record,* 78 (Dec. 1976):563.

Theft and Mutilation of Books and Materials

BAHR, ALICE HARRISON. *Book Theft and Library Security Systems, 1981–82.* White Plains: Knowledge Industry Publications, 1981.

———. "Electronic Security for Books." *Library Trends,* 11 (Summer 1984):29–38.

BERRY, JOHN N., III. "To Catch a Thief." *Library Journal,* 90 (April 1965):1617–21.

GANDERT, SLADE R. "Protecting Your Collection." *Library and Archival Security,* 4 (1982):1–137.

JENKINS, JOHN H. *Rare Book and Manuscript Thefts, A Security System for Libraries, Booksellers and Collectors.* New York: Antiquarian Booksellers Assn. of America, 1982.

KATZENSTEIN, HERBERT. "Guidelines for the Security of AV Equipment." *Library Security Newsletter,* 1 (July 1975):9.

KNIGHT, NANCY H. "Library Security Systems Come of Age." *American Libraries,* 9 (April 1978):229–32.

———. "Theft Detection Systems for Libraries Revisted, An Updated Survey." *Library Technology Reports,* 15 (May–June 1979):219–413.

KRASKE, NEAL K. "Moffitt Undergraduate Library Book Loss Study." *Library Security Newsletter,* 2 (Spring 1976):6–7.

LINCOLN, ALAN JAY, and CAROL ZALL LINCOLN. "The Impact of Crime in Public Libraries." *Library and Archival Security,* 3 (Fall/Winter 1980):125–34.

MASON, PHILIP P. "Archival Security: New Solutions to an Old Problem." *American Archivist,* 38 (Oct. 1975):477–92.

MAST, SHARON. "Ripping Off and Ripping Out: Book Theft and Mutilation from

Academic Libraries." *Library and Archival Security,* 5 (Winter 1983):31–50.

PEARSON, L. R. "Former Library Director Begins Jail Term." *American Libraries,* 7 (Oct. 1976):554.

PETERSEN, NANCY H. "Upping the Ante on Overdues." *Library and Archival Security,* 3 (Spring 1980):25.

SHERIDAN, R. N. "Measuring Book Disappearance: How to Evaluate the Need for Collection Protection." *Library Journal,* 99 (Sept. 1974):2040–3.

Fire Protection

ANDERSON, B. E. "Ordeal at Santa Fe State College." *Library Journal,* 95 (April 1970):1275–80.

BRYAN, JOHN L. *Automatic Sprinkler and Standpipe Systems.* Boston: National Fire Protection Assn., 1971.

BUSH, STEPHEN E. "Libraries and Museum Collections." In *The Fire Protection Handbook,* 15th ed., pp. 68–84. Quincy, Mass.: National Fire Protection Assn., 1981.

CHICARELLO, PETER, et al. *Fire Tests on Mobile Storage Systems for Archival Storage.* Norwood: Factory Mutual Research, 1978.

COHEN, WILLIAM. "Case Study in Library Arson." *Library and Archival Security,* 2 (Spring 1976):3.

DOWLING, J. H., and CHARLES BURTON FORD. "Halon 1301 Total Flooding System for Winterthur Museum." *Fire Journal,* 63 (Nov. 1969):10–14.

DYKINS, JEANNE. "The Youngstown Library Fire: A Crime against the People." *Library and Archival Security,* 2 (1978):20–22.

EASTWOOD, C. R., et al. "Fire!" *Library Association Record,* 80 (Sept. 1978):455.

HARVEY, BRUCE. "Sprinkler Systems and Books." *Library Journal,* 99 (July 1974):1741.

KENNEDY, JOHN. "Library Arson." *Library and Archival Security,* 2 (Spring 1976):1–3.

LAWTON, WILLIAM N. "The Use of Fast-Acting Sprinklers—Experience in the U.S.A.," unpublished, an address before the London International Fire Conference, April 10, 1984.

MORRIS, JOHN. "Current Fire Protection Topics." *Professional Safety,* 20 (Feb. 1975):60–63.

———. "Is Your Library Safe from Fire?" *American School and University,* 52 (April 1980):60–63.

———. *Managing the Library Fire Risk.* 2nd ed. Berkeley: Univ. of California, 1979.

———. "Protecting the Library from Fire." *Library Trends,* 33 (Summer 1984):49–56.

NATIONAL FIRE PROTECTION ASSOCIATION, Quincy, Mass., *National Fire Codes* (current editions):

    #10   *Portable Fire Extinguishers*
    #12A *Halon 1301 Fire Extinguishing Systems*
    #12B *Halon 1211 Fire Extinguishing Systems*

    #13 *Installation of Sprinkler Systems*
    #910 *Protection of Libraries and Library Collections*
    #911 *Protection of Museums and Museum Collections*
    #101 *The Life Safety Code*
THOMPSON, ROBERT J. "The Decision Tree for Fire Safety Systems Analysis: What It Is and How to Use It." *Fire Journal,* 69 (July, Sept., Nov. 1975).
WILLEY, A. E. "The Charles Klein Law Library Fire." *Fire Journal,* (Nov. 1972):16–22.

Water Damage: Protection and Recovery
BUCHANAN, SALLY, and PHILIP D. LEIGHTON. *The Stanford Lockheed-Meyer Library Flood Report.* Stanford, Calif.: Stanford Univ. Libraries, 1980.
DARLING, PAMELA W. "Beset by Foes on Every Side." In *Disasters, Prevention and Coping,* pp. 18–23. Stanford, Calif.: Stanford Univ. Libraries, 1981.
LEIGHTON, PHILIP D. "Reducing Preservation Hazards Within Library Facilities." In *Disasters, Prevention and Coping,* pp. 32–40. Stanford, Calif.: Stanford Univ. Libraries, 1981.
RUGGERE, CHRISTINE, and E. H. MORSE. "The Recovery of Water-Damaged Books at the College of Physicians in Philadelphia." *Library and Archival Security,* 3 (Fall/Winter 1980):23–28.
SCHMELZER, MENAHEM. "Fire and Water: Book Salvage in New York and in Florence." *Special Libraries,* 59 (Oct. 1969):620–25.
STEINMETZ, WILLIAM H. "How a Campus Handles an Earthquake Disaster." *Proceedings, 26th National Conference on Campus Safety.* Chicago: National Safety Council, 1979.
WATERS, PETER. "1972 Flood Disasters: Lessons for the Future." *Library Journal,* 98 (Feb. 1973):490.
———. *Procedures for Salvage of Water-Damaged Library Materials.* Washington, D.C.: Library of Congress, 1975.

Planning and Design for Safety and Security
BRANNIGAN, FRANCIS L. *Building Construction for the Fire Service.* Boston: National Fire Protection Assn., 1971.
DREYFUSS, HENRY. *Designing for People.* New York: Simon and Schuster, 1955.
JENSEN, ROLF. *Fire Protection for the Design Professional.* Boston: Cahners Publishing Co., 1975.
LANGMEAD, STEPHEN, and MARGARET BECKMAN. *New Library Design: Guidelines to Planning Academic Library Buildings,* 28. Toronto: Wiley, 1970.
MASON, ELLSWORTH. *Mason on Library Buildings.* Metuchen, N.J.: Scarecrow Press, 1980.
METCALF, KEYES D. *Planning Academic and Research Library Buildings.* New York: McGraw-Hill, 1965.
POOLE, WILLIAM F. "Construction of Library Buildings." *Library Journal,* 6 (April 1981):69.
THOMPSON, GODFREY. *Planning and Design of Library Buildings.* 2nd ed. London: Architectural Press Ltd., 1973.

Toffler, Alvin. "Libraries." In *Bricks and Mortarboards.* New York: Educational Facilities Laboratories, Inc., 1964.

Watts, Ellen. "The Mayer Art Center of the Phillips Exeter Academy: An Engaging Combination of Adaptive Reuse and New Construction." *Technology and Conservation,* 7 (Fall 1982):20–21.

Preservation and Conservation

Banks, Paul N. "Cooperative Approaches to Conservation." *Library Journal,* 101 (Nov. 1976):2348–51.

———. "Environmental Standards for Storage of Books and Manuscripts." *Library Journal,* 99 (Feb. 1974):339–43.

———. "Preservation of Library Materials." *Encyclopedia of Library and Information Science.* Vol. 23. Pittsburgh: Univ. of Pittsburgh, 1978.

Blades, William. *The Enemies of Books.* London: Trübner and Co., 1880.

Brandt, Charles A. E. "Care and Storage of Works on Paper." *Library and Archival Security,* 5 (Spring 1983):1–10.

Cunha, George Martin. "The Care of Books and Documents." In *Codicologica 5, Les matériaux du livre manuscrit,* pp. 59–78. Leiden: E. J. Brill, 1980.

———, and Dorothy Grant Cunha. *Conservation of Library Materials, A Manual and Bibliography on the Care, Repair and Restoration of Library Materials.* 2nd ed. Metuchen, N.J.: Scarecrow Press, 1971.

———. *Library and Archives Conservation: 1980s and Beyond.* Metuchen, N.J.: Scarecrow Press, 1983.

Darling, Pamela W. "Local Preservation Program: Where to Start." *Library Journal,* 101 (Nov. 1976):2343–47.

———. "Our Fragile Inheritance: The Challenge of Preserving Library Materials." *ALA Yearbook,* 1976, pp. xxxi–xlii. Chicago: American Library Assn., 1977.

———. "Will Anything Be Left? New Approaches to the Preservation Challenge." *Wilson Library Bulletin,* 56 (Nov. 1981):177–81.

Morrow, Carolyn Clark. *Conservation Treatment Procedures.* Littleton, Colo.: Libraries Unlimited, 1982.

———, and Gay Walker. *The Preservation Challenge.* White Plains, N.Y.: Knowledge Industry Publications, 1983.

Nelson, Milo. "Evening the Odds: The Northeast Document Conservation Center." *Wilson Library Bulletin,* 56 (Nov. 1981):187–91.

Poole, Frazer G. "The Proposed National Preservation Program of the Library of Congress." *Library Journal,* 101 (Nov. 1976):2351.

Russell, Ann "The Northeast Document Conservation Center: Case Study in Cooperative Conservation." *American Archivist,* 45 (Winter 1982):45–52.

Schmidt, J. David. "Freeze Drying of Historic Cultural Properties: Valuable Process in Restoration and Documentation." *Technology and Conservation,* 9 (Spring 1985):21–26.

Schur, Susan E. "Conservation Profile, the Northeast Document Conservation Center." *Technology and Conservation,* 7 (Fall 1982):34–39.

Swartzburg, Susan G. *Preserving Library Materials.* Metuchen, N.J.: Scarecrow Press, 1980.

WALKER, GAY. "The Quiet Disaster II." In *Disasters, Prevention and Coping,* pp. 24–31. Stanford, Calif.: Stanford Univ. Libraries, 1981.

WEINSTEIN, FRANCES RUTH. "A Psocid by any other name . . . is still a pest." *Library and Archival Security,* 6 (Spring 1984):57–63.

Insurance and Risk Management

ADAMS, J. F. *Risk Management and Insurance: Guidelines for Higher Education.* Washington, D.C.: National Assn. of College and Univ. Business Officers, 1972.

Best's Loss Control Engineering Manual (revised annually). Oldwick, N.J.: A. M. Best and Co., 1984.

KENNEWEG, RICHARD. "Developing a Library Insurance Program." *Library Security Newsletter,* 2 (Spring 1976):11–14.

MYERS, GERALD E. *Insurance Manual for Libraries.* Chicago: American Library Assn., 1977.

School District Insurance Handbook. Chicago: Illinois Association of School Business Officials, Risk Management Committee, 1985.

TRELLES, OSCAR M. "Protection of Libraries." *Law Library Journal,* 66 (Aug. 1973):241–58.

Index

Prepared by Gene Heller

127

John Morris lives in Walnut Creek, California. He served six years as a loss control consultant assigned to the University of California, and before that held similar responsibilities at the universities of Illinois and Minnesota. A graduate of Bowdoin College, he belongs to ALA, the American Society of Safety Engineers and the National Fire Protection Association, and is an active member of NFPA's Committee on Libraries, Museums and Historic Buildings. Morris is the author of *Managing the Library Fire Risk* (University of California, 1975, 1979). He has contributed to such publications as *Library Trends, Library & Archival Security, National Safety News, Professional Safety, Fire Journal, American School and University,* and two British journals, *Library Association RECORD* and *Fire Prevention.*